AN ILLUSTRATED GUIDE TO
MODERN
TANKS
AND FIGHTING VEHICLES

a **Salamander** book

Published by Arco Publishing, Inc.
NEW YORK

AN ILLUSTRATED GUIDE TO
MODERN
TANKS
AND FIGHTING VEHICLES

A Salamander Book

Published by
Arco Publishing, Inc.,
215 Park Avenue South,
New York,
N.Y. 10003,
United States of America.

©1980 by Salamander Books Ltd.,
27 Old Gloucester Street,
London WC1N 3AF,
United Kingdom.

Library of Congress catalog card
number 80-65165

ISBN 0-668-04965-0

Contents

Combat vehicles are arranged in numerical and/or alphabetical order of
their common designations.

Credits

Consultant; Christopher F. Foss, author of and contributor to many technical reference books concerned with armoured fighting vehicles.

Editor: Ray Bonds
Designer: Lloyd Martin

Colour drawings:
© Salamander Books Ltd., and
© Profile Publications Ltd.

Photographs: The publishers wish to thank all the official international governmental archives, weapons systems manufacturers and private collections who have supplied photographs for this book.

Printed in Belgium by Henri Proost et Cie.

122mm M1974
Self-propelled Howitzer

Country of origin: Soviet Union.
Crew: 4.
Armament: One 122mm howitzer.
Armour: Classified.
Dimensions: Length 23ft 11in (7.3m); width 9ft 10in (3.005m); height 7ft 11in (2.42m).
Weight: (combat) 35,280lbs (16,000kg).
Engine: YaMZ-238 V-8 diesel developing 2400hp at 2100rpm.
Performance: Road speed 37mph (60kmh); road range 310 miles (500km); vertical obstacle 3ft 3in (1m); trench 9ft 9in (3m); gradient 60 per cent.
History: Entered service with Soviet Union in early 1970s, also in service with Czechoslovakia, East Germany and Poland.

The 122mm M1974 self-propelled howitzer was one of two new Soviet self-propelled artillery pieces to be introduced into service in the early 1970s, the other being the 152mm M1973. The hull is of all welded and (possibly aluminium construction.

The layout of the M1974 is similar to that of the M1973 with the driver seated towards the front on the left, engine and transmission to the right and the turret well towards the rear of the hull. To the immediate front of the driver is a windscreen that can be covered by an armoured shutter hinged at the top when the vehicle is in a combat area, and over the top of the driver's position is a single piece hatch cover that opens to the rear. The commander is seated on the left side of the turret and has a cupola that can be traversed ʳough a full 360° and is provided with a single piece hatch cover that opens ιo the front, forward of which are periscopes and an infra-red search light that can be operated by the commander from within the turret. The gunner is seated forward and below the commander and the loader on the right side of the turret, with a single piece hatch cover that opens forwards.

The suspension is of the torsion bar type and consists of seven rubber

Below: The M-1974 armed with a 122mm howitzer.

Above: The M1974 was first paraded in Poland in July 1974.

tyred road wheels with the drive sprocket at the front and idler at the rear; there are no track return rollers.

Main armament consists of a modified version of the 122mm D-30 towed howitzer and is fitted with a double baffle muzzle brake and a fume extractor. This fires an HE projectile weighing 48.06lbs (21.8kg) with a maximum muzzle velocity of 690 metres a second to a maximum range of 16,738 yards (15,300m), and a rocket assisted projectile is also thought to have been developed with a range of some 22,974 yards (21,000m). The weapon can also fire a fin-stabilised HEAT projectile weighing 31.09lbs (14.1kg), which has a muzzle velocity of 809 yards a second (740 metres a second) and at a range of 1094 yards (1000m) will penetrate 18in (460mm) of armour at an incidence of 0°. A total of 40 rounds of ammunition are carried and maximum rate of fire for a short period is five rounds per minute. The weapon has an elevation of +70° and a depression of −3°; turret traverse is 360°.

The M1974 is fully amphibious, being propelled in the water by its tracks at a speed of 3mph (4.5kmh) and, unlike in most other Soviet amphibious vehicles, a trim vane is not fitted to stop water rushing up the glacis plate when the vehicle is afloat. The M1974 is fitted with an NBC system.

152mm M1973
Self-propelled Gun/Howitzer

Country of origin: Soviet Union.
Crew: 5.
Armament: One 152mm gun/howitzer; one 7.62mm anti-aircraft M.G.
Armour: Classified.
Dimensions: Length (with armament) 25ft 6in (7.78m); length (hull) 23ft 5in (7.14m); width 10ft 6in (3.2m); height (turret top) 8ft 11in (2.72m).
Weight: Combat 61,600lbs (28,000kg).
Engine: 500hp diesel.
Performance: Road speed 34mph (55kmh); road range 310 miles (500km); vertical obstacle 3ft 3in (1m); trench 9ft 2in (2.8m); gradient 60 per cent.
History: Entered service with Soviet Union in early 1970s. In production. (Note: the above specifications are provisional).

During the 1960s the Soviets realised that the introduction by the West of ATGWs posed a serious threat to their tanks and the development of self-propelled guns was rapidly pushed ahead.

The 152mm M1973 is now being introduced into Soviet units on the scale of 18 per division. The layout of the M1973 is similar to that of the American 155mm M109 self-propelled howitzer with the engine and transmission at the front of the hull and the large turret towards the rear. The driver is seated towards the front of the vehicle on the left and has a single piece hatch cover that opens to his rear; to his immediate front are periscopes for forward observation when the hatch is closed.

The large turret has a single hatch in the right side and a cupola for the vehicle commander is provided on the left side of the turret roof. The commander's cupola has a single piece hatch cover that opens to the rear and is provided with vision devices, a 7.62mm machine-gun is mounted on the forward part of the cupola and it is possible that this can be aimed and fired from within the vehicle. The indirect sight is mounted in the turret roof forward of the commander's position with the direct sight being mounted to the left of the main armament. An ammunition resupply hatch is provided in the rear of the hull but, unlike in the American M109, there are no spades at the rear of the hull to absorb recoil when the weapon is fired. The suspension is of the torsion bar type and consists of six dual rubber tyred road wheels with the drive sprocket at the front, idler at the rear and four track return rollers.

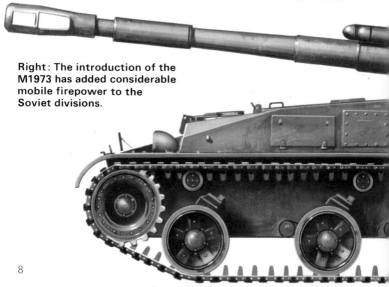

Right: The introduction of the M1973 has added considerable mobile firepower to the Soviet divisions.

Above: The 152mm self-propelled gun/howitzer M-1973 was seen in public for the first time during November 1977 Moscow parade.

Main armament consists of a 152mm gun/howitzer which is a development of the towed 152mm D-20 gun/howitzer, the ordnance being provided with a double baffle brake and a fume extractor. When travelling the ordnance is held in position by a travel lock which folds back onto the glacis plate when not required. The weapon has an elevation of +56° and a depression of −3° and the turret can be traversed through a full 360°. The M1973 can fire an HE projectile weighing 96.13lbs (43.6kg) to a maximum range of 26,256 yards (24,000m) and unconfirmed reports have spoken of a rocket assisted projectile with a range of 40,478 yards (37,000m). An APHE projectile weighing 107.6lbs (48.8kg) can also be fired; this will penetrate 5in (130mm) of armour at a range of 1,094 yards (1000m). A total of 40 projectiles are carried and the maximum rate of fire is four rounds per minute; in the sustained fire role average rate of fire is two rounds per minute.

The M1973 can ford to a depth of 4ft 11in (1.5m) without preparation but unlike the 122mm M1974 has no amphibious capability. A full range of night driving equipment is installed as is an NBC system.

155mm Bandkanon 1A Self-propelled Gun

Country of origin: Sweden.
Crew: 5.
Armament: One 155mm gun; one 7.62mm anti-aircraft machine-gun.
Armour: 20mm (0.79in) maximum.
Dimensions: Length (overall) 36ft 1in (11m); length (hull) 21ft 6in (6.55m); width 11ft 1in (3.37m); height (with anti-aircraft MG) 12ft 8in (3.85m).
Weight: Combat 116,850lbs (53,000kg).
Ground pressure: 12lb/in^2 (0.85kg/cm^2).
Engines: One Rolls-Royce K.60 diesel developing 240hp at 3,750rpm, and one Boeing Model 502/10MA gas turbine developing 300shp at 38,000rpm.
Performance: Road speed 17mph (28km/h); range 143 miles (230km); vertical obstacle 3ft 2in (0.95m); trench 6ft 7in (2m); gradient 60 per cent.
History: Entered service with Swedish Army in 1966, production completed in 1968. Still in service.

The *Bandkanon* 1A, or VK-155 as it is also known, is one of the heaviest self-propelled guns in service anywhere in the world. The prototype was built by the famous Bofors Ordnance Company in 1960, but the type was not produced in large numbers, staying in production for only two years. The VK-155 shares many automotive components with the S-Tank, for example the power pack, which was also designed and built by Bofors. The driver is

continued ▶

Above: The 155mm gun of the Bandkanon 1A has a maximum elevation of +40° and a depression of –3°, and is mounted in a fully armoured turret which can be traversed 15° left and 15° right.

Left: Many of the automotive components of the 155mm Bandkanon 1A are identical to those of the S tank which was also designed and manufactured by the famous Bofors company for the Swedish Army.

seated in the front part of the hull whilst the other four crew members are seated in the large turret at the rear of the hull. The 155mm gun has an elevation of +40° and a depression of −3°, and traverse is 15° left and 15° right. Elevation and traverse are both powered, but manual controls are provided for use in an emergency. The gun is fed from a magazine which holds 14 rounds in two layers of seven rounds, allowing the weapon to achieve a high rate of fire — a complete magazine in one minute. Once the magazine is empty a full magazine is brought up by a truck and loaded in place of the empty magazine, which takes about two minutes. The 155mm gun fires its HE round to a maximum range of 23,410 yards (21,400m). As soon as the weapon has fired the required number of rounds it would normally move to a new fire position before the enemy could pinpoint its exact position and return fire. A 7.62mm machine-gun is mounted on the left side of the turret, and can be used against both ground and air targets. The chassis has six road wheels, with the drive sprocket at the front. The suspension,

which is of the hydro-pneumatic type, is locked in position when the gun is fired, thus providing a more stable firing platform. Although a unique gun, the VK-155 has a number of drawbacks. It is very heavy, rather slow and difficult to move across some bridges and roads. It is not possible to change types of ammunition quickly. For example, a forward observer may ask for five rounds of HE on a target, followed by smoke rounds. But unless the magazine has a smoke round at that time it would not be able to comply. Moreover, unlike most other Swedish AFVs, for example the S-Tank, the Pbv.302 APC and the lkv.91 tank destroyer, the VK-155 has no amphibious capability at all. Sweden is not going to build any more self-propelled guns of this type, and instead has designed a new towed weapon, the 155mm FH77, now in production at Bofors.

Below: 155mm Bandkanon showing the magazine at the rear which holds 14 HE rounds in two layers of seven rounds.

155mm Mk F3
Self-propelled Howitzer

Country of origin: France.
Crew: 2 (+ 8 with accompanying vehicle).
Armament: One 155mm howitzer.
Armour: 0.4–0.8in (10–20mm).
Dimensions: Length (with armament) 20ft 5in (6.22m); width 8ft 11in (2.72m); height 6ft 10in (2.1m).
Weight: (combat) 38,367lbs (17,400kg).
Ground pressure: 0.8kg/cm^2.
Engine: SOFAM 8-cylinder petrol developing 250hp at 3200rpm.
Performance: Road speed 40mph (65kmh); range 186 miles (300km); vertical obstacle 2ft (0.6m); trench 4 ft 11in (1.5m); gradient 50 per cent.
History: Entered service with the French Army in 1960s. In service with Argentina, Chile, Ecuador, France, Kuwait, United Arab Emirates and Venezuela.

The 155mm Self-Propelled Howitzer MkF3 was developed by the Atelier de Construction de Tarbes (armament) and the Atelier de Construction Roanne (chassis). Production was undertaken by Creusot-Loire.

The chassis is all of welded steel construction with the driver seated

Above: The 155mm self-propelled howitzer Mk F3 is essentially a shortened AMX-13 light tank chassis with a 155mm howitzer mounted at the rear of the hull. It is now being replaced in the French Army by the 155mm GCT.

Right: 155mm self-propelled howitzer Mk F3 with weapon at maximum elevation. The driver and commander ride on the vehicle and the remainder of the gun crew and ammunition follow in an AMX VCA tracked vehicle.

towards the front on the left and the vehicle commander to his rear; the engine is to the right of the driver and the 155mm howitzer is mounted at the rear. The suspension is of the well tried torsion bar type and consists of five rubber tyred road wheels with the drive sprocket at the front and the last road wheel acting as the idler, and two track return rollers. The first and last road wheel stations have a hydraulic shock absorber.

The MkF3 is basically a shortened AMX-13 tank chassis with the 155mm howitzer mounted at the rear. When travelling the howitzer is in the horizontal position and locked 8° to the right of the vehicle's centre line. The weapon has a double baffle muzzle brake and can be elevated from 0° to +67°, traverse is 20° left and 30° right (with an elevation of 0 to +50°) and 16° left and 30° right (with an elevation from +50 to +67°).

Two of the crew, the driver and commander, ride with the self-propelled howitzer, with the other eight members of the gun crew following in an AMX VCA tracked vehicle which carries 25 projectiles, 25 charges and fuses. The howitzer has a maximum rate of fire of three rounds per minute, although when being used in the sustained fire role this drops to about one round per minute. The ammunition is of the separate loading type, ie projectile and charge, and the following types can be fired: HE projectile weighing 96.46lbs (43.75kg), range 21,880 yards (20,000m), hollow base projectile weighing 95.36lbs (43.25kg), range 23,630 yards (21,600m), illuminating projectile weighing 97.02lbs (44kg), range 19,418 yards (17,750m), smoke projectile weighing 97.57lbs (44.25kg), range 19,418 yards (17,750m) and a rocket assisted projectile weighing 93.71lbs (42.5kg), range 25,162 yards (23,300m).

155mm SP-70
Self-propelled Howitzer

Country of origin: International.

In the 1960s, three NATO countries, Britain, West Germany and the United States, all agreed that they required a new 155mm towed howitzer to replace weapons dating back to World War II. Eventually the United States went on to develop a towed howitzer under the designation of the XM198. Britain and West Germany went ahead and developed the 155mm FH-70 which, unlike the American M198, has an auxiliary power unit which enables it to propel itself around the battery position. For the FH-70 project Britain was the project leader and in 1970 Italy joined the project as an equal partner. There are three production lines for the FH-70, one in each country, with components being supplied by one country to the other two: Britain builds the carriage, West Germany the ordnance and Italy the cradle. First production FH-70s were delivered in 1978.

In 1973 development of the self-propelled version of the FH-70 commenced under the designation of the SP-70 with West Germany the project leader. A total of 12 prototypes of the SP-70 are being built: West Germany are responsible for the ordnance (Rheinmetall), powerpack (MTU) and chassis (MaK), Italy responsible for the cradle, recoil system, elevating and balancing equipment (OTO-Melara), and Britain responsible for the turret, ammunition handling system and the sighting system (Royal Armament Research and Development Establishment designed the turret and the prototypes were completed by the Royal Ordnance Factory at Leeds).

Trials with the prototypes are expected to continue until the early 1980s and it is not expected that the SP-70 will enter service until the mid-1980s at the earliest. The British Army will replace its 105mm Abbot and 155mm M109s with the SP-70 while in the West German and Italian Armies it will replace M109s. Main improvements over the M109 will be a much increased

SP-70 is a joint development between Britain, West Germany and Italy and will replace the 155mm M109 in these countries.

Above: Britain is responsible for the turret of the 155mm SP-70.

range and a high rate of fire, necessary against fast-moving enemy tanks.

Prototypes of the SP-70 are based on automotive and suspension components of the Leopard 1 MBT which is in widespread use by NATO forces, including West Germany and Italy. The hull of the SP-70 is of all welded aluminium construction with the driver's compartment in the front, turret in the centre and the engine and transmission at the rear. The suspension system is of the torsion bar type and consists of seven dual rubber tyred road wheels with the idler at the front, drive sprocket at the rear and four return rollers.

The 155mm weapon is mounted in the forward part of the turret and has a large double baffle muzzle brake and a fume extractor, and the balancing cylinders either side of the ordnance are housed in armoured housings. Turret traverse and gun elevation are powered and manual controls are provided for emergency use. To enable a high rate of fire to be achieved SP-70 is fitted with an automatic loading system; no details of the rate of fire have been released but it is probable that between six and eight rounds a minute can be fired. Once the ammunition supply has been expended SP-70 would move to a predetermined position for ammunition resupply, with ammunition loaded through two doors in the rear of the turret.

The ammunition system of the SP-70 is identical to that of the FH-70 and consists of three projectiles and a charge system. The three projectiles weigh 94.8lbs (43.5kg) each and are HE, base ejection smoke (DM105) and illuminating (DM106); they can be fired to a maximum range of 21,880 yards (20,000m). In addition all standard NATO 155mm projectiles can be fired including the recent Martin Marietta Copperhead Cannon Launched Guided Projectile. Under development is a Rocket Assisted Projectile which will have a maximum range of 32,760 yards (30,000m). The charge system has eight zones and is divided into three separate cartridges, zones 1–2, 3–7, and 8.

A41 Centurion Main Battle Tank

Country of origin: Britain.

Crew: 4.

Armament: One 105mm L7 series gun; .3in machine-gun co-axial with main armament; one .5in ranging machine-gun; one .3in machine-gun on commander's cupola; six smoke dischargers on each side of the turret.

Armour: 17–152mm (0.67–6.08in).

Dimensions: Length (gun forward) 32ft 4in (9.854m); length (hull) 25ft 8in (7.823m); width (including skirts) 11ft 1½in (3.39m); height 9ft 10½in (3.009m).

Weight: Combat 114,250lbs (51,820kg).

Ground pressure: 13.5lb/in² (0.95kg/cm²).

Engine: Rolls-Royce Meteor Mk IVB 12-cylinder liquid-cooled petrol engine developing 650bhp at 2,550rpm.

Performance: Road speed 21.5mph (34.6km/h); range 118 miles (190km); vertical obstacle 3ft (0.914m); trench 11ft (3.352m); gradient 60 per cent.

History: Entered service with the British Army in 1949. The Centurion is still used by Denmark, India, Israel, Jordan, the Netherlands, Kuwait, South Africa, Sweden, Switzerland and Britain (artillery observation role).

The Centurion was developed from 1944 by the AEC company of Southall, Middlesex, under the designation A41 cruiser. Six prototypes were com-

Below: The
Centurion was
designed towards
the end of World
War II but remains
in service even today.

Below: Centurion Armoured Vehicle Royal Engineers carrying a
length of rolled aluminium roadway and towing a trailer.

Left: 105mm armed Centurion tanks of the Israeli Army on the
Golan Heights in 1973. Israeli Army is now the largest user of the
tank, most of which have now been fitted with diesel engines.

pleted by the end of the war but arrived in Germany too late to see any
combat. Centurion production was undertaken by the Royal Ordnance
Factory at Leeds, Vickers Limited at Elswick and Leyland Motors of Leyland.
Total production amounted to some 4,000 tanks and late production
models cost about £50,000. The Centurion has seen combat in Korea, India,
South Arabia, Vietnam, the Middle East and Suez and has proved to be one
of the outstanding vehicles developed since World War II. Although designed
over 30 years ago, the Centurion is still an effective fighting vehicle. One of
the reasons why it has been so successful is that it has proved capable of
being upgunned and uparmoured to meet the latest requirements. The only ▶

Above: Centurion tank of the Swedish Army armed with 105mm L7 tank gun. 350 Centurions were purchased by Sweden in the 1950s.

drawback of the Centurion has been its slow speed and its poor operational range. Early models had a range of only 65 miles (104km) and various methods of increasing this were tried, including the fitting of fuel drums on the rear of the hull, but these were prone to damage when the tank was travelling across country, and were also a fire hazard. The Mk 5 could tow a jettisonable mono-wheel armoured trailer which carried another 200 gallons (909 litres) of fuel. Later models had additional fuel which increased operating range to 118 miles (190km). The Centurion was replaced in the British Army from 1967 by the Chieftain MBT, and a modified Centurion (the FV4202) had been used in the development of the Chieftain. The Centurion was to have been replaced by the so-called Universal Tank in the early 1950s, but this programme was dropped, the only thing to come out of it being the FV214 Conqueror. The Centurion has a hull of all-welded steel construction, with a turret of cast armour with the top welded into position. The driver is seated at the front of the hull on the right, with the other three crew members in the turret, the commander and gunner on the right and the loader on the left. The engine and transmission are at the rear of the hull. The engine is a development of the Rolls-Royce Merlin aircraft engine which was used to power the World War II Spitfire and Hurricane fighters. The suspension is of the Horstmann type, and each side has three units, each of these having two road wheels. The drive sprocket is at the rear and the idler at the front, and there are six track-return rollers. The top half of the tracks and suspension are covered by armoured track skirts, providing some measure of protection against HEAT attack. The last model of the Centurion was the Mk 13, a modified Mk 10. In all there have been no less than 25 marks of the Centurion gun tank. The Mk 13 is armed with the famous L7 series 105mm gun, which has an elevation of +20° and a depression of −10°, in a turret with 360° traverse. The gun is fully stabilised in both elevation and traverse. A .3in machine-gun is mounted co-axially with the main armament, and there is a similar weapon on the commander's cupola. A .5in ranging machine-gun is provided and there are six smoke dischargers on each side of the turret. Some 64 rounds of 105mm, 600 rounds of .5in and 4,750 rounds of .3in ammunition are carried. When first introduced into service the Centurion had no night-vision equipment, but later marks have infra-red driving lights and an infra-red

Above: Centurion tank armed with a 20 pounder gun in action with the Royal Australian Armoured Corps in Vietnam. Australia now uses the Leopard 1 MBT.

searchlight mounted to the left of the main armament. The Centurion can ford to a depth of 4ft 6in (1.45m) without preparation, and although many amphibious kits were developed, none of these was adopted. The Centurion has also served as the basis for a whole range of vehicles. Two bridgelayers were developed, both of them based on the Mk 5 hull. The FV4002 has a bridge which is kept in the horizontal position when travelling; this is swung vertically through 180° to be laid into position. The ARK (FV4016) bridgelayer itself enters the gap, whereupon ramps are opened out at each end. The ARK could be used to span gaps of up to 75ft (22.86m) in width. The FV4002 is no longer used by the British Army and the FV4016 has now also been withdrawn from service. The Mk 2 ARV (FV4006) was the standard Army Recovery Vehicle of the British Army but has now been replaced by the Chieftain ARV although it remains in service with a number of overseas armies including Israel, Sweden and Switzerland. The FV4006 has a winch with a maximum capacity of 90 tons (91,445kg) and spades are provided at the rear of the hull. The type has a crew of four and is armed with a .3in machine-gun. The Beach Armoured Recovery Vehicle (BARV) is capable of operations in water up to 9ft 6in (2.895m) in depth. The Armoured Vehicle Royal Engineers (AVRE) or FV4003 is armed with a 165mm demolition gun and also has a dozer blade at the front of the hull; if required it can tow a trailer with the Giant Viper mine-clearance equipment. There have also been many trials models, including a 25-pounder self-propelled gun (this had a Centurion chassis with five road wheels) a 5.5in self-propelled gun, the Conway 120mm tank-destroyer, and a 180/183mm tank-destroyer. Many armies have modified the tank to meet their own specific requirements. The Israelis have fitted a Centurion with a new turret mounting a 155mm gun, but this has not yet entered service. Israel has also rebuilt many of its Centurions with 105mm guns, new American Continental diesel engines, new transmissions and many other modifications. Vickers are offering a refit kit for the Centurion, including a new diesel, semi-automatic transmission, and a new cupola.

AMX-GCT Self-propelled Gun

Country of origin: France.
Crew: 4.
Armament: One 155mm gun; one .7.62mm anti-aircraft machine-gun; four smoke dischargers.
Armour: 50mm (1.96in) maximum, estimated.
Dimensions: Length (with gun forward) 33ft 2in (10.2m); length (hull) 21ft 3in (6.485m); width 10ft 4in (3.15m); height (without anti-aircraft MG) 10ft 10in (3.3m).
Weight: 92,610lbs (42,000kg).
Ground pressure: 12.8lb/in^2 (0.9kg/cm^2).
Engine: Hispano-Suiza HS-110 12-cylinder multi-fuel engine developing 720hp at 2,400rpm.
Performance: Road speed 37mph (60km/h); range 280 miles (450km); vertical obstacle 3ft 3in (0.93m); trench 6ft 3in (1.9m); gradient 60 per cent.
History: Entered service with French Army in 1979, also in service with one country in the Middle East. In production.

At the present time the standard self-propelled artillery of the French Army consists of .105mm and 155mm weapons on modified AMX-13 type chassis. It was decided some years ago that both of these weapons would be replaced by a new 155mm weapon as the current weapon of this calibre, the Mk.F3, has a number of drawbacks: the gun cannot be traversed through a full 360°, the gun is on an open mount with no protection for the crew against small arms fire and NBC attack, and it has to be supported in action by a modified AMX armoured personnel carrier for the rest of the crew and the ammunition for the gun. The four main requirements laid down by the French Army were: mobility similar to that of a main battle tank, ability to engage targets quickly through a full 360° at all ranges, high rate of fire with effective ammunition, and full protection for the crew from both NBC attack and small arms fire. The first prototype of the GCT (*Grande Cadence de Tir*) was completed in 1973; further models followed two years later, and the type is now in production for the French Army. The GCT consists of a slightly modified AMX-30 main battle tank chassis with a new turret of all-welded steel construction. The crew of four consists of the commander, driver and two gunners (one of the gunners is in charge of the fire-control system and elevation and traverse of the main armament, whilst the other prepares the charges and controls the loading of the gun). The main armament consists of a 155mm gun with a double baffle muzzle-brake, capable of an elevation of +66° and a depression of −4°, traverse being a full 360° Elevation and traverse are hydraulic, with manual controls in case of hydraulic failure. The gun is fully automatic and can fire eight rounds in one minute. A total of 42 projectiles and their separate bagged charges is carried in the rear of the turret, arranged in seven racks of six for both projectiles and bags. The propelling charges are contained in combustible cases so that the crew does not have to worry about empty cases littering the floor of the turret. A typical ammunition load would consist of 36 High Explosive and six Smoke rounds. Large doors are provided in the rear of the turret for reloading purposes, and it takes three men about 30 minutes to reload the ammunition. Types of ammunition fired included High Explosive. Smoke and Illuminating, of both French and American manufacture. The HE round has a maximum range of 26,256 yards (24,000m), although a rocket-assisted round with a range of 34,461 yards (31,500m) is now being developed. A 7.62mm anti-aircraft machine-gun is mounted on top of the turret, with traverse through a full 360° and elevation limits from −20° to +50°. Some 2,000 rounds of 7.62mm ammunition are carried. In addition there are two smoke dischargers on each side of the turret. The GCT is provided with an NCB system, and night-vision equipment can be fitted if required. The vehicle can ford to a depth of 6ft 10in (2.1m) without preparation. As the crew may well have to remain in the vehicle for up to 24 hours at a time, a bunk has been installed in the turret to allow one member of the crew to rest. Whilst the introduction of the GCT will increase the effectiveness of the French artillery arm, it is considered by some to be too expensive and too heavy when compared with other self-propelled guns such as the American M109. On the credit side, the ability to fire a large number of rounds in a short space of time is of vital importance on the battlefield of the 1980s. This is because once an SP gun has fired one round, enemy gun-locating radars will start to pin-point its exact position, and within a few minutes the enemy will be returning fire. The role of the GCT will be to fire a burst of eight rounds and then move to a new firing position before the enemy counter-fire arrives.

Left: 155mm GCT SPG from the rear with its ammunition resupply hatches lowered to show ammunition racks for 42 projectiles (eg., 36 HE and 6 smoke) and 42 charges. Four men can reload the GCT within 20 minutes.

Below: 155mm GCT SPG with turret traversed to the rear. It is the first SPG in NATO to have an automatic loading system which enables it to fire eight projectiles per minute to a maximum range of 26,256 yards (24,000m).

AMX-13 Light Tank

AMX-13, ARV, AVLB and variants
Country of origin: France.
Crew: 3.
Armament: One 75mm gun; one 7.5mm or 7.62mm machine-gun co-axial with main armament; two smoke dischargers on each side of the turret.
Armour: 10 to 40mm.
Dimensions: Length (gun forward) 20ft 10in (6.36m); length (hull) 15ft (4.88m); width 8ft 2in (2.5m); height 7ft 7in (2.3m).
Weight: Combat 33,069lbs (15,000kg).
Ground pressure: 10.81lb/in² (0.76kg/cm²).

Below: Spectacular firing of an SS.11 anti-tank missile from AMX-13 Model 51 armed also with 75mm gun.

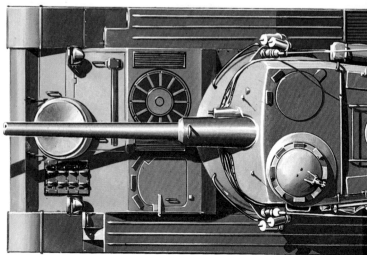

Engine: SOFAM Model 8 GXb eight-cylinder water-cooled petrol engine developing 250hp at 3,200rpm.

Performance: Road speed 37mph (60km/h); range 218 miles (350km); vertical obstacle 2ft 2in (0.65m); trench 5ft 3in (1.6m); gradient 60 per cent.

History: Entered service with the French Army in 1953–54. Also used by Algeria, Argentina, Chile, Djibouti, Dominican Republic, Ecuador, El Salvador, India, Indonesia, Ivory Coast, Morocco, the Netherlands, Nepal, Peru, Saudi Arabai, Singapore, Switzerland, and Tunisia. No longer used by Austria, Cambodia, Egypt, Israel, Lebanon and Vietnam and will be phased out of service with the Netherlands and Switzerland in the next few years.

The AMX-13 was one of the three armoured vehicles developed by the French after the end of World War II, the others being the Panhard EBR-75 armoured car and AMX-50 heavy tank. The AMX-13 was designed by the ▶

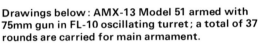

Drawings below: AMX-13 Model 51 armed with 75mm gun in FL-10 oscillating turret; a total of 37 rounds are carried for main armament.

Atelier de Construction d'Issy-les-Moulineaux near Paris and the first proto-type was completed in 1948–49, which in itself was quite an achievement. The type entered production at the *Atelier de Construction* Roanne in 1952 and production continued at this plant until the early 1960s, when production was transferred to the Creusot-Loire plant at Chalons-sur-Saône. The AMX-13 is still in production and by 1979 over 10,000 AMX-13 type vehicles, including tanks, self-propelled guns, and APCs had been built. The AMX-13 was designed for use as a tank destroyer or reconnais-sance vehicle and is still the standard light tank of the French Army. The hull is all-welded steel construction and has a maximum thickness of 1.575in (40mm). The driver is seated at the front of the hull on the left, with the engine to his right. The turret is towards the rear of the hull, with the com-mander on the left and the gunner on the right. The suspension is of the torsion-bar type and there are five road wheels, with the idler at the rear and the drive sprocket at the front. There are two or three track-return rollers. To keep the height of the tank as low as possible the French designed the tank for crew members with a maximum height of 5ft 8in (1.727m). The turret is of the French-designed oscillating type and has two parts. The lower part is mounted on the turret ring and has two trunnions on which upper part, the top of the turret (together with the gun) is mounted. On this type of installa-tion the top of the turret is elevated or depressed complete with the gun, which is fixed. The fitting of a turret of this type enabled the French to install an automatic loader, and this in turn reduced the crew to three as a crew member was not required for loading purposes. The gun is fed from two revolver-type magazines, each of which holds six rounds of ammunition, giving a total of 12 rounds for ready use. The empty cartridge cases are

Below: This AMX-13 has a 105mm gun which fires a HEAT projectile that can penetrate 360mm of armour at an incidence of 0° at 1,000m.

Above: AMX-13 being refuelled in the field. It has seen combat in both the Middle and Far East and is still in production.

ejected automatically through a hole in the rear of the turret. Once the 12 ready rounds have been expanded, the magazines have to be reloaded from outside of the turret. A 7.5mm or 7.62mm machine-gun is mounted co-axially with the main armament and there are two smoke dischargers on each side of the turret. The oscillating turret is also fitted to the Panhard 8 x 8 EBR heavy armoured car, the Austrian *Panzerjäger* tank destroyer and the Brazilian EE-17 Sucuri tank destroyer. The first AMX-13s to enter service were armed with a 75mm gun which fired either HE or HEAT rounds. The latter would penetrate 6.7in (170mm) of armour at a range of 2,187 yards (2,000m). The next model had a slightly different oscillating turret and was armed with a 105mm gun, firing a HEAT round which would penetrate 14.17in (360mm) of armour. This model was not adopted by the French Army, but was purchased by the Netherlands. Some fatigue problems were encountered when the type first entered service. All AMX-13s in use with the French Army today have been refitted with a new 90mm gun firing fin-stabilised rounds, 34 rounds of 90mm and 3,600 rounds of machine-gun ammunition being carried. The AMX-13 can ford to a depth of 2ft (0.6m) without preparation, but has no amphibious capability. When it first entered service the AMX-13 did not have any night-vision equipment, but most have now been fitted with infra-red driving lights and some also have an infra-red searchlight mounted on the turret. France was one of the first countries to make use of wire-guided anti-tank missiles; and many AMX-13s have been fitted with two SS-11 missiles on each side of the main armament to give them long-range anti-tank capability. Some years ago an AMX-13 was fitted with the HOT missile system, three missiles being mounted in their launcher boxes on each side of the turret. This model was not adopted, however, and the French Army is now developing a special version of the AMX-10P MICV armed with the HOT system. The basic AMX-13 tank was followed by the AMX VCI armoured personnel carrier and the 105mm Mk.61 self-propelled howitzer. Both of these have their own entries, and so are not described here. The bridgelayer version, or *Char Poseur de Pont*, is provided with a scissors type bridge which can be laid over the rear of the hull. When in position this allows tanks weighing up to 23.62 tons (24,000kg) to cross ditches and other obstacles; two of these bridges can be laid side by side so that an AMX-30 MBT can use them. The *Char de Depannage* is the armoured recovery version. This is fitted with an 'A' frame pivoted at the front of the hull and swinging back on to the rear of the hull when not required. It can be used to change engines and trans-missions. When this 'A' frame is being used, the front suspension can be locked to provide a more stable platform. Two winches are provided, the main one having a capacity of 15.75 tons (16,000kg). Four spades are mounted at the rear of the hull. The ARV has a crew of three. Armament consists of a 7.5mm or 7.62mm machine-gun and smoke dischargers. Without doubt the AMX-13 has been one of the most successful tank designs since World War II and has given birth to a whole range of vehicles which can only be equalled by the Russian PT-76 light tank and the American M113 families.

AMX-30 Main Battle Tank

AMX-30, ARV, AVLB, SPAAG and variants
Country of origin: France.
Crew: 4.
Armament: One 105mm gun; one 20mm cannon or one 12.7mm machine-gun co-axial with main armament (see text); one 7.62mm machine-gun on commander's cupola; two smoke dischargers on each side of turret.
Armour: 50mm (1.96in) maximum, estimated.
Dimensions: Length (including main armament) 31ft 1in (9.48m); length (hull) 21ft 8in (6.59m); width 10ft 2in (3.1m); height (including searchlight) 9ft 4in (2.85m).
Weight: Combat 79,366lbs (36,000kg).
Ground pressure: 10.95lb/in² (0.77kg/cm²).
Engine: HS-110 12-cylinder water-cooled multi-fuel engine developing 720hp at 2,600rpm.
Performance: Speed 40mph (65km/h); range 373 miles (600km); vertical obstacle 3ft 1in (0.93m); trench 9ft 6in (2.9m); gradient 60 per cent.
History: Entered service with the French Army in 1967. Also in service with Greece, Iraq, Libya, Peru, Saudi-Arabia, Spain and Venezuela.

After the end of World War II France quickly developed three vehicles, the AMX-13 light tank, the Panhard EBR 8 x 8 heavy armoured car and the AMX-50 heavy tank. The last was a very interesting vehicle with a hull and suspension very similar to the German PzKpfw V Panther tank used in some numbers by the French Army in the immediate postwar period. The AMX-50 had an oscillating turret, a feature that was also adopted for the AMX-13

tank. The first AMX-50s had a 90mm gun, this being followed by a 100mm and finally a 120mm weapon. At one time it was intended to place the AMX-50 in production, but as large numbers of American M47s were available under the US Military Aid Program (MAP) the whole programme was cancelled. In 1956 France, Germany and Italy drew up their requirements for a new MBT for the 1960s. The basic idea was good: the French and Germans were each to design a tank to the same general specifications; these would then be evaluated together; and the best tank would then enter production in both countries, for use in all three. But like many international tank programmes which were to follow, this came to nothing: France placed her AMX-30 in production and Germany placed her Leopard 1 in production. The AMX-30 is built at the *Atelier de Construction* at Roanne, which is a government establishment and the only major tank plant in France. The first production AMX-30s were completed in 1966 and entered service with the French Army the following year. The type has now replaced the American M47 in the French Army and has also been exported to a number of countries. No total production figures have been released but it is estimated that about 2,000 AMX-30s have been built so far. The hull of the AMX-30 is of cast and welded construction, whilst the turret is cast in one piece. The driver is seated at the front of the hull on the left, with the other three crew members in the turret. The commander and gunner are on the right of the turret with the loader on the left. The engine and transmission are at the rear of the hull, and can be removed as a complete unit in under an hour. Suspension is of the torsion-bar type and consists of five road wheels, with the drive sprocket at the rear and the idler at the front, and there are five track-return rollers. These support the inner part of the track. The main armament of the AMX-30 is a 105mm gun of French design and manufacture, with an elevation of +20° and a depression of −8°, and a traverse of 360°, both elevation and

Below: The AMX-30 is the standard MBT of the French Army and is manufactured at the Atelier de Construction Roanne where the AMX-10P MICV and AMX-10RC recce vehicles are also built.

Below: The AMX-30S has been developed specifically for desert operations and has been ordered by at least one country in the Middle East. Modifications include the fitting of sand shields, modified engine, and transmission which reduces speed to 60kmh.

traverse being powered. A 12.7mm machine-gun or a 20mm cannon is mounted to the left of the main armament. This installation is unusual in that it can be elevated independently of the main armament to a maximum of 40°, enabling it to be used against slow flying aircraft and helicopters. There is a 7.62mm machine-gun mounted on the commander's cupola and this can be aimed and fired from within the turret. Two smoke dischargers are mounted each side of the turret. 47 rounds of 105mm, 500 rounds of 20mm and 2,050 rounds of 7.62mm ammunition are carried. There are five types of ammunition available for the 105mm gun: HEAT, HE, Smoke, Illuminating and Practice. The HEAT round is the only anti-tank round carried. This weighs 48.5lbs (22kg) complete, has a muzzle velocity of 3,281 feet per second (1,000m/s) and will penetrate 14.17in (360mm) of armour at an angle of 0°. Most other tanks carry at least two, and often three, different types of anti-tank ammunition, for example HESH, APDS and HEAT. The French HEAT round is of a different design to other HEAT rounds and the French claim that it is sufficient to deal with any type of tank it is likely to encounter on the battlefield. Other HEAT projectiles spin rapidly in flight as they are fired from a rifled tank gun, but the French HEAT round has its shaped charge mounted in ball bearings, so as the outer body of the projectile spins rapidly, the charge itself rotates much more slowly. In 1980 an APFSDS projectile will enter production, and this will be able to penetrate 1.96in (50mm) of armour at an incidence of 60° and a range of 5,470 yards (5,000m). The AMX-30 can ford streams to a maximum depth of 6ft 7in (2m) without preparation. A schnorkel can be fitted over the loader's hatch, and this enables the AMX-30 to ford to a depth of 13ft 2in (4m). Infra-red driving equipment is fitted, as is an infra-red searchlight on the commander's cupola and another such searchlight to the left of the main armament. An NBC system is fitted as standard equipment. The latest model

Above: Mounted to the left of the main armament is a Sopelem PH-8-B searchlight which has a range of 800m in infra-red mode.

of the AMX-30 to enter production for the French Army is the AMX-30 B2 which has a number of modifications including a much improved fire control system. Further development has resulted in the AMX-32 for which there is a separate entry. For export the AMX-30 can be delivered without NBC or night-vision equipment and with a much simpler cupola. A special model has been developed for use by Saudi-Arabia, this being known as the AMX-30S. It has a laser rangefinder, sand shields and a modified trans-mission. There are a number of experimental models of the AMX-30 type and the following models are already in production or in service. The

Above: A much modified AMX-30 MBT chassis is used as the transporter/launcher for the Pluton tactical nuclear missile.

AMX-30D is the armoured recovery vehicle and has a crew of four (commander, driver and two mechanics). Equipment fitted includes a dozer blade at the front of the hull, a crane (hydraulically operated) and two winches, one with a capacity of 34.45 tons (35,000kg) and the other with a capacity of 3.94 tons (4,000kg). Armament consists of a cupola-mounted 7.62mm machine-gun and smoke dischargers. The bridgelayer version carries a scissor type bridge which, opened out, can span a gap of up to 65ft 7in (20m); this model has a crew of three (commander, bridge operator and driver). The AMX-30 has also been modified to carry and launch the French-developed Pluton tactical nuclear missiles. The missile is elevated for launching and has a maximum range of 62 miles (100km). This model is now in service with the French Army and has replaced the American-supplied Honest John missiles. An anti-aircraft gun tank is now in production for Saudi-Arabia, armed with twin 30mm cannon and fitted with an all-weather fire-control system. This has not been adopted by the French Army as it already uses the AMX-13 anti-aircraft tank with a similar turret. There is a separate entry for the 155mm GCT self-propelled gun. Saudi-Arabia has also ordered an anti-aircraft missile system called the Shahine, a development of the Crotale missile system which is now in service with the French Air Force and a number of other armies. One AMX-30 vehicle carries six missiles in the ready-to-launch position, as well as the launch radar, whilst another tank has the search and surveillance radar. The French Army has modified the AMX-30 to carry the Roland SAM system: two missiles are carried in the ready-to-launch position with a further eight missiles inside the hull. Roland has been developed by France and West Germany with the former responsible for the clear weather Roland 1 and the latter responsible for the all weather Roland 2. Roland is also in service with Brazil (on the West German Marder chassis), has been ordered by Norway and is being manufactured in the United States under licence.

AMX-32 Main Battle Tank

Country of origin: France.
Crew: 4.
Armament: One 105mm gun; one 20mm cannon co-axial with main armament; one 7.62mm anti-aircraft machine-gun; six smoke dischargers.
Armour: Classified.
Dimensions: Length (with armament) 31ft 1in (9.48m); length (hull) 21ft 7in (6.59m); width 10ft 7in (3.24m); height 9ft 8in (2.96m).
Weight: (combat) 83,790lbs (38,000kg).
Ground pressure: $0.85kg/cm^2$.
Engine: Hispano-Suiza HS 110 12-cylinder multi-fuel developing 720hp at 2000rpm.
Performance: Road speed 40mph (65kmh); road range 329 miles (530km); vertical obstacle 3ft (0.93m); trench 9ft 6in (2.9m); gradient 60 per cent.
History: Prototype completed in 1979. Not yet in production.

Most second generation MBTs such as the American M1 (XM1), West German Leopard 2 and British Shir 2 are characterised by a size and weight which make them unsuitable for employment in many parts of the world, even if their manufacturers were allowed to sell them on the world market. A classic recent example is the West German Leopard 1, which has only been sold to NATO countries, apart from Australia, and prospective buyers in the Middle East and elsewhere have been forced to look elsewhere and have usually ended up buying French or Soviet equipment. France has exported large numbers of AMX-30 MBTs to countries that include Greece, Iraq, Libya, Peru, Saudi Arabia, Spain and Venezuela.

Rather than develop a new tank for the early 1980s the French Army elected to carry out a mid-life modernisation programme to its existing AMX-30 tank fleet (in a similar manner to the British Army's policy in updating their Chieftains so that they will remain effective through the 1980s until the arrival of MBT-80). The modernised AMX-30 is known as the AMX-30 B2 and is basically an AMX-30 with the automatic COTAC integrated fire-control system, LLLTV system, new transmission and a new collective pressurisation system.

For the export market the AMX-32 has been developed; this was announced in 1977 and the first prototype was unveiled in June 1979. At the

Above: The AMX-32 MBT derives from the AMX-30 and has been developed by France specifically for the export market, but will not be produced until a firm order has been received.

time of writing no country had placed an order for the tank although several countries are said to be very interested. The AMX-32 is a further development of the AMX-30 B2 but has increased armour protection which improves the tank's chances of survival when encountering ATGWs and other infantry anti-tank weapons fitted with HEAT warheads.

The hull of the AMX-32 like that of the AMX-30 is of rolled steel plates welded together with the driver's compartment at the front, fighting com- ▶

Below: The AMX-32 has the same armament and fire control system as the latest version of the AMX-30, the AMX-30 B2, but has a new all-welded turret which offers additional armour protection and more room for the crew.

Above: The AMX-32 has a 105mm gun which traverses with the turret through 360° and has an elevation of −8° to +20°.

partment in the centre and the engine at the rear. The nose and glacis plate are of cast and welded construction rather than cast construction as in the case of the AMX-30. The driver is seated on the left side and has a single piece hatch cover that opens to the left, in front of which are three periscopes for forward observation when driving with the hatch closed. The driver steers the tank with a steering wheel rather than two sticks as in the case of most other tanks.

The turret of the AMX-32 is all of welded construction and offers both increased protection and more room for the crew than the AMX-30 turret. The commander is seated on the right of the turret with the gunner forward and below his position. The commander's cupola has periscopes for all round observation and mounted in its roof is a stabilised sight which enables him to lay and fire the main armament or designate the target for the gunner and then resume his primary role of commanding the tank. This sight has a magnification of x2 or x8 in the day mode and x1 in the night mode. The gunner has an optical sight with a magnification of x10 and a laser range-finder. Mounted to the right of the mantlet is a LLLTV camera which moves in elevation with the main armament and provides a picture to both the commander's and gunner's TV monitor screens. The integrated COTAC fire control system gives the tank a high hit probability under both day and night conditions. The loader is seated on the left of the turret and has a single piece hatch cover that opens to the rear and periscopes for observation. In the left side of the turret is an ammunition resupply hatch.

The engine is identical to that installed in the AMX-30 and AMX-30 B2 tanks and the transmission is the same as that installed in the latter. The transmission is composed of a hydraulic torque converter, electrohydraulic-ally controlled gearbox with five forward gears and a reverser, and a hydro-static steering system. This enables the driver to change gear under torque, carry out pivot turns, change gears while turning and reduces driver fatigue and training.

The suspension is similar to that of the AMX-30 but the torsion bars, shock absorbers, and bump stops have been strengthened to take account of the increased weight and mobility of the tank. The upper parts of the tracks are now covered by armoured skirts which hinge upwards for maintenance and give protection against HEAT attack.

Main armament is identical to that of the AMX-30 but provision has been made to replace this with a new French 120mm smooth bore gun which can

fire the same ammunition as the West German Leopard 2. In addition to the rounds described in the entry for the AMX-30 the AMX-32 can also fire the recent French APFSDS projectile, which when complete weighs 12.78lbs (5.8kg) with the penetrator weighing 7.93lbs (3.6kg), and has a muzzle velocity of 143 yards a second (130 metres a second) and will penetrate 6in (150mm) of armour at an incidence of 60°. Mounted co-axially to the left of the main armament is a 20mm M693 F2 cannon which can be linked to the main armament or elevated independently to +40° to enable it to be used against low flying helicopters. A 7.62mm machine-gun is mounted on the commander's cupola and this can be aimed and fired from within the tank. Three electrically operated smoke dischargers are mounted either side of the turret. A total of 47 rounds of 105mm, 500 rounds of 20mm and 2050 rounds of 7.62mm machine-gun ammunition are carried.

If the AMX-32 is placed in production it will be manufactured at the Atelier de Construction Roanne where production of the AMX-30 tank family and AMX-10P MICV family is undertaken.

Below: View from rear clearly shows ammunition resupply case to left of turret. Loader has access to it from inside turret.

AMX 105mm Self-propelled Gun

Mk.61 (Obusier de 105 Model 1950 sur Affût Automoteur) fixed and turreted models

Country of origin: France.

Crew: 5.

Armament: One 105mm howitzer; one 7.5mm anti-aircraft machine-gun.

Armour: 10mm–20mm (0.40–0.79in).

Dimensions: Length 21ft (6.4m); width 8ft 8in (2.65m); height (with cupola) 8ft 10in (2.7m).

Weight: Combat 36.376lbs (16,500kg).

Ground pressure: 11.38lb/in² (0.8kg/cm²).

Engine: SOFAM 8 GXb eight-cylinder water-cooled petrol engine developing 250hp at 3,200rpm.

Performance: Road speed 37.28mph (60km/h); range 218 miles (350km); vertical obstacle 2ft (0.65m); trench 6ft 3in (1.9m); gradient 60 per cent.

History: Entered service with the French Army in 1952. Still in service with France, Morocco and the Netherlands. No longer in production.

This self-propelled 105mm gun was the first vehicle to be developed from the AMX-13 light tank chassis. The initial prototype was completed in 1950, with production vehicles following in 1952. The type remains in service with the French Army, although both this and the 155mm Mk.F3 self-propelled weapon are to be replaced by the 155mm GCT self-propelled gun in the next five years. In the 1950s most armies had both 105mm and 155mm self-propelled weapons, but over the past 10 years the 105mm self-propelled gun has been dropped as the 155mm round is much more effective. The Mk.61's chassis is similar to that of the AMX-13 light tank, although it is higher at the back. The driver is seated at the front of the hull on the left with the engine to his right. The other four crew members are the commander, gunner and two loaders, located in the gun compartment at the rear of the hull, which is of all-welded construction with a maximum armour thickness of 0.8in (20mm). The gun has an elevation of +70° and a depression of −4.5°, traverse being limited to 20° left and 20° right. Both elevation and traverse are manual. One of the drawbacks of this weapon is that it cannot be quickly laid on to a new target, as would a gun mounted

Below: The 105mm Mk.61 SPG was the first of many vehicles to be developed based on the chassis of the AMX-13 light tank.

Above: 105mm Mk.61 SPG in firing position with an AMX battery command vehicle to the rear; the latter is also a member of the AMX-13 family of AFVs, of which some 10,000 have been built.

in a turret with a traverse of 360°. Two barrels were developed for the weapon, one of 23 calibres and the other of 30 calibres. (The term calibre in this context indicates the length of the gun barrel from the breech ring to the muzzle measured in terms of the gun's bore: for example the 105mm gun has a 23 calibre barrel, so its length is 23 times the calibre of 105mm, which equals 7ft 11in or 2.415m.) Both barrels are provided with a double-baffle muzzle-brake, whose primary purpose is to retard the force of recoil: as the projectile leaves the muzzle, the gases driving it strike the baffles of the muzzle-brake and are deflected to the sides and rear; the gases exert a forward force on the baffle that partially counteracts the rearward force of recoil. Fifty-six rounds of ammunition are normally carried, including six anti-tank rounds. The HE projectile weighs 35.27lbs (16kg) and has a maximum range of 16,404 yards (15,000m), muzzle velocity being from 772 to 2,198fps (220 to 670m/s). The fire control equipment consists of a x 6 telescope for anti-tank operations and a goniometer with a magnification of x 4. Most vehicles have a 7.5mm anti-aircraft machine-gun on the roof for anti-aircraft defence. Some vehicles are fitted with a turret-mounted 7.5mm machine-gun with a traverse of 360°. The vehicle's suspension is similar to that of the AMX-13 light tank and consists of five road wheels, with the drive sprocket at the front and the idler at the rear; there are three track-return rollers. Shock absorbers are provided for the first and fifth road wheels. This model does not have an NBC system and has no amphibious capability, although it can ford streams to a depth of 2ft 8in (0.8m). The Mk.61 was followed in the late 1950s by a model with a similar gun in a turret with a traverse of 360°, the gun having an elevation of +70° and a depression of −7°. Eighty rounds of ammunition were carried, including six for anti-tank use. A 7.5mm anti-aircraft machine-gun was mounted in a cupola on the roof of the turret. This had full traverse through 360° and could be elevated from −15° to +45°. Total combat weight was 17 tons and crew of five. The type was tested by the French and Swiss armies but was not adopted. Other self-propelled weapons on AMX-13 chassis include the AMX-13 DCA with twin 30mm anti-aircraft guns and the 155mm Mk.F3 self-propelled gun both of which are in service with the French Army.

ASU-57 Self-propelled Anti-tank Gun

Country of origin: Soviet Union.
Crew: 3.
Armament: One 57mm gun.
Armour: 0.32in (6mm).
Dimensions: Length (with armament) 16ft 5in (4.995m); length (hull) 11ft 5in (3.48m); width 6ft 10in (2.086m); height 3ft 10in (1.18m).
Weight: (combat) 7387lbs (3350kg).
Ground pressure: 0.35kg/cm².
Engine: Model M-20E 4 cylinder petrol developing 55hp at 3600rpm.
Performance: Road speed 28mph (45kmh); range 155 miles (250km); vertical obstacle 1ft 8in (0.5m); trench 4ft 7in (1.4m); gradient 60 per cent.
History: Entered service with Russian Army in mid-1950s. In service with Egypt, Soviet Union and Yugoslavia. Production complete.

The ASU-57 was developed in the 1950s specifically for use by the Soviet Airborne Divisions and was seen in public for the first time during a parade held in Red Square, Moscow, in 1957. The ASU-57 (ASU being the Soviet designation for airborne assault gun and 57 for the calibre of the gun, 57mm) is issued on the scale of 54 per Airborne Division, with each of the division's three parachute regiments having one battalion consisting of three six-gun batteries. The An-12 transport aircraft can carry two ASU-57s for air dropping, each being dropped on an air-drop platform to which large parachutes are attached. Shortly before the platform hits the ground, retro-rockets are fired so reducing the effect of impact.

To save weight, the ASU-57 is all of aluminium construction with the engine at the front and the open topped crew compartment at the rear. The driver is seated to the right of the main armament with the gunner seated on the left. The suspension is of the torsion bar type and consists of four rubber tyred road wheels with the drive sprocket at the front, two track return rollers and the last road wheel acting as the idler.

Main armament consists of a long barrelled 57mm gun which is offset slightly to the left of the vehicle's centre line; the first model of the ASU-57 to enter service was armed with the Ch-51 gun which can be distinguished by its long multi-slotted muzzle brake, while the later, and more common, Ch-51M gun has a much shorter barrel and a double baffle muzzle brake. When travelling the barrel is secured by a triangular-shaped lock. The gunner aims the 57mm gun with an OPZ-50 optical sight and the gun itself has an elevation of +12°, a depression of −5° and a traverse of 8° left and 8° right, both elevation and traverse being manual. The gun, which is a development of the famous 57mm M1943(ZIS-2) anti-tank gun of the Second World War has a semi-automatic vertical sliding breech block and a well trained crew can fire ten rounds a minute.

The 57mm gun fires ammunition of the fixed type. The APHE projectile

Right: Front and side drawings of the ASU-57 self-propelled anti-tank gun clearly show the low profile of the vehicle. Its thin armour makes it vulnerable to most weapons on the battlefield.

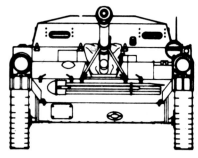

Above: The ASU-57 entered service with Soviet airborne units in the 1950s and is issued on the scale of 54 per division.

weighs 6.8lbs (3.1kg), has a muzzle velocity of 321 feet a second (980 metres a second) and will penetrate .33in (85mm) of armour at a range of 1094 yards (1000m). The HE projectile weighs 6.2lbs (2.8kg), has a muzzle velocity of 761 yards a second (685 metres a second) and a maximum range of 6673 yards (6100m). The HVAP projectile weighs 4lbs (1.8kg), has a muzzle velocity of 761 yards a second (695 metres a second) and will penetrate 4in (100mm) of armour at a range of 1094 yards (1000m). A total of 30 rounds of 57mm ammunition are carried; some vehicles also carry a 7.62mm machine gun for use in the ground role.

The thin armour of the ASU-57 provides the three man crew with protection from rifle and light machine gun fire only and its open top makes the crew vulnerable from artillery bursts. The vehicle has no NBC equipment and no amphibious capability and will probably be phased out of service in the not too distant future.

Above: An ASU-57 with 57mm Ch-51M gun advances across the snow with infantry support during a winter training exercise.

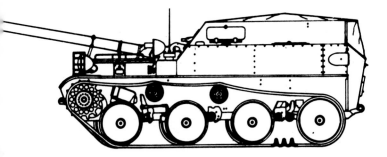

ASU-85 Self-propelled Anti-tank Gun

Country of origin: Soviet Union.
Crew: 4.
Armament: One 85mm gun; one 7.62mm PKT machine-gun co-axial with main armament; one 7.62mm anti-aircraft machine-gun.
Armour: 10mm—40mm (0.39—1.57in).
Dimensions: Length (with armament) 27ft 10in (8.49m); length (hull) 19ft 8in (6m); width 9ft 2in (2.8m); height 6ft 11in (2.1m).
Weight: Combat 30,865lbs (14,000kg).
Ground pressure: 6.25lb/in² (0.44kg/cm²).
Engine: Model V-6 six-cylinder inline water-cooled diesel developing 240hp at 1,800rpm.
Performance: Road speed 27.3mph (44km/h); range 162 miles (260km); vertical obstacle 3ft 8in (1.1m); trench 9ft 2in (2.8m); gradient 70 per cent.
History: Entered service with the Russian Army in 1961. In service with East Germany, Iran (doubtful if delivered) and the Soviet Union. Production completed about 1964.

Above: The 85mm gun of the ASU-85 has a fume extractor and a double baffle muzzle brake. The APHE projectile weighs 20.5lbs (9.3kg), has a muzzle velocity of 2598ft/s (792m/s) and will penetrate 102mm of armour at a range of 1093 yards (1000m); the HVAP projectile will penetrate 130mm of armour at this range.

The ASU-85 is issued on the scale of 18 per airborne rifle division. These have two drawbacks. First they have very thin armour and no overhead protection at all, and secondly their 57mm gun is not adequate against tanks. Each Russian airborne regiment has a battery of nine ASU-57s, whilst each airborne division has a battalion of 18 ASU-85s. The ASU-85 (ASU is the abbreviation for *Aviadezantnaya Samochodnaya Ustanovka*, and the 85 refers to the size of the main armament) is normally transported in the Antonov An-12 'Cub' transport aircraft and can be air-dropped. For air-dropping the vehicle is mounted on a platform to which are attached a number of parachutes. Just before the platform reaches the ground a number of retro-rockets are fired to reduce the platform's velocity so that no damage occurs. The ASU-85 has a hull of all-welded steel construction which varies in thickness from 0.4in (10mm) on the hull roof to 1.57in (40mm) on the glacis and mantlet. The fighting compartment is at the front, with the engine and transmission at the rear. Many components of the ASU-85 are taken from the PT-76 amphibious light tank family. The crew consists of commander, gunner, loader and driver, the last being seated at the front of the vehicle on the right ▶

 Left: Main armament of the ASU-85 consists of an 85mm gun mounted in the forward part of the hull. This fires fixed APHE, HE and HVAP rounds and has an elevation of +15°, depression of −4° and total traverse of 12°.

Below: Mounted over the main armament of the ASU-85 at the rear is an infra-red searchlight; a smaller one is mounted forward of the commander's position to the right of the 85mm gun and this can be operated safely from within the vehicle.

side. The ASU-85 has torsion-bar suspension and a total of six road wheels with the idler at the front and the drive sprocket at the rear, but does not have any track-return rollers. The 85mm gun is provided with a double baffle muzzle-brake and a fume extractor, and is mounted slightly offset to the vehicle's left; traverse is a total of 12° and elevation from −4° to +15°. A 7.62mm PKT machine-gun is mounted co-axially with the main armament. A total of 40 rounds of 85mm ammunition is carried, including HE, APHE and HVAP. The HE projectile weighs 20.9lbs (9.5kg) and has a muzzle velocity of 2,598ft/s (792m/s), the APHE projectile weighs 20.5lbs (9.3kg) and also has a muzzle velocity of 2,598ft/s, and the HVAP projectile weighs 11.02lbs (5kg) and has a muzzle velocity of 3,379ft/s (1,030m/s). The APHE round will penetrate 4in (102mm) of armour at a range of 1,093 yards (1,000m) whilst the HVAP round will penetrate 5.12in (130mm) of armour at a similar range. The ASU-85 is believed to be fitted with an NBC system. Infra-red driving lights are fitted and there is an infra-red searchlight over the main armament and another in front of the commander's hatch, the last controllable from within the vehicle. The vehicle does not have any amphibious capability, although it can ford to a depth of 3ft 8in (1.1m) without preparation. Two fuel drums can be attached to the rear of the hull to increase operational range.

Left: An ASU-85 being un-
loaded from a Soviet aircraft.
It is airportable in the An-12
(Cub) and is issued on the
scale of 18 per Soviet airborne
division; it is also used by
East Germany and possibly Iran.

Below: The ASU-85 was
developed in the late 1950s
and was seen in public for the
first time during a parade
held in Moscow in 1962. It
uses many parts of the PT-76
light tank family but, unlike
this vehicle, is not amphibious.

FV433 Abbot
Self-propelled Gun

Country of origin: Britain.
Armament: One 105mm gun; one 7.62mm light machine-gun for anti-aircraft defence; two three-barrelled smoke dischargers.
Armour: 6mm–12mm (0.24–0.47in).
Dimensions: Length overall 19ft 2in (5.84m); width 8ft 8in (2.641m); height 8ft 2in (2.489m).
Weight: Combat 36,500lbs (16,556kg).
Ground pressure: 12.65lb/in² (0.89kg/cm²).
Engine: Rolls-Royce K.60 Mk.4G six-cylinder multi-fuel engine developing 240bhp at 2,750rpm.
Performance: Road speed 30mph (48km/h); water speed 3.1mph (5km/h); range 242 miles (390km); vertical obstacle 2ft (0.609m); trench 6ft 9in (2.057m); gradient 60 per cent.
History: Entered service with British Army in 1964. No longer in production. Value Engineered Abbot is in service with Indian Army.

Self-propelled artillery was first used by the British Army as far back as 1927, and during World War II the advantages of SP artillery became even more apparent. During the war the British Army used a variety of self-propelled guns (SPGs), including the Bishop (25-pounder on a Valentine chassis), the Sexton (25-pounder on a Ram chassis) and the American Priest (105mm on a Sherman chassis). After the war various experimental self-propelled guns were built. In the 1950s it was decided to use the FV430 chassis as the basis for both an APC and an SPG. The first prototype of the SPG, designated FV433, was completed in 1961. Production was undertaken at the Vickers works at Elswick, Newcastle-upon-Tyne, between 1964 and 1967. The FV433, called the Abbot, is in service with medium regiments of ▶

Right: Abbot 105mm self-propelled gun with gun at maximum elevation; it fires a 16.1kg HE projectile to a range of 17,000m.

Below: Top and rear views of Abbot self-propelled gun which has many automotive components of the FV432 family of tracked APCs.

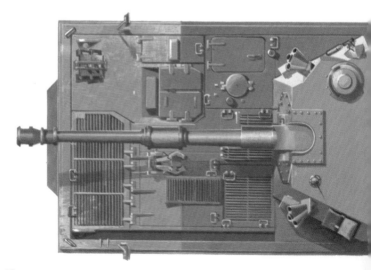

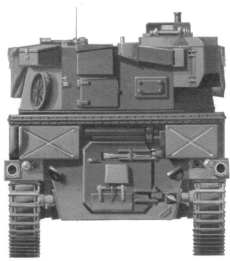

the Royal Artillery in Britain, and in Germany with the British Army of the Rhine. Each regiment normally has three batteries each with six Abbots, usually supported in action by the 6 x 6 Alvis Stalwart load carrier to supply additional ammunition. The Abbot has a crew of four. The driver is seated at the front of the hull and the other three crew members are seated in the turret. The turret is mounted at the rear of the hull and has full power traverse through 360°. The 105mm gun has an elevation of from −5° to +70°. The gun fires separate-loading ammunition of the following types: High Explosive, Smoke Base Ejection, Target Indicating, Illuminating, Squash Head Practice and High Explosive Squash Head, the last being for use against tanks. The gun has a maximum range of 15,550 yards (14,220m). A 7.62mm Bren light machine-gun is mounted on the roof for anti-aircraft defence, and in addition smoke dischargers are mounted each side of the turret. Forty rounds of 105mm and 1,200 rounds of 7.62mm ammunition are carried. A flotation screen is carried collapsed around the top of the hull. This can be erected in 10 to 15 minutes, and the Abbot can then propel itself across rivers with its tracks at a maximum speed of 3mph (5km/h). The Abbot is provided with an NBC system and infra-red driving lights for night driving. There were two variants of the Abbot. This first was the Value Engineered Abbot, in service with the Indian Army. This was essentially a standard Abbot with such things as the NBC system and flotation screen removed. The second was the Falcon twin 30mm self-propelled anti-aircraft gun which never progressed beyond the prototype stage.

Below: Abbot is deployed with the British Royal Artillery both in Britain and with the British Army of the Rhine in Germany.

Above: Abbot with flotation screen stowed which, when erected, enables it to propel itself across rivers by its tracks at 3mph (5km/h).

FV4201 Chieftain Main Battle Tank

FV4201 MBT, FV4204 ARV, FV4205 AVLB. Shir Iran
Country of origin: Britain.
Crew: 4.
Armament: One 120mm L11 series gun; one 7.62mm machine-gun co-axial with main armament, one 7.62mm machine-gun in commander's cupola; one .5in ranging machine-gun; six smoke dischargers on each side of turret.
Armour: Classified.
Dimensions: Length (gun forward) 35ft 5in (10.795m); length (hull) 24ft 8in (7.518m); width overall (including searchlight) 12ft (3.657m); height overall 9ft 6in (2.895m).
Weight: Combat 121,250lbs (55,000kg).
Ground pressure: 14,22lb/in^2 (0.9kg/cm^2).
Engine: Leyland L.60 No 4 Mk 8A 12-cylinder multi-fuel engine developing 750bhp at 2,100rpm.
Performance: Road speed 30mph (48km/h); road range 280 miles (450km); vertical obstacle 3ft (0.914m); trench 10ft 4in (3.149m); gradient 60 per cent.
History: Entered service with the British Army in 1967 and also used by Iran and Kuwait.

In the 1950s the British Army issued a requirement for a new tank to replace the Centurion tank then in service. The army required a tank with improved firepower, armour and mobility. The Chieftain was designed by the Fighting Vehicles Research and Development Establishment (now the Military Vehicles and Engineering Establishment), and the first prototype was completed in 1959. The Chieftain (FV4201) was preceded by a tank known as the FV4202, however. This was designed by Leyland; and two of them were built and used to test a number of features later adopted for the Chieftain. The FV4202 used some Centurion automotive components. The Chieftain prototype was followed by a further six prototypes in 1961–62, and after more development work the Chieftain was accepted for army use in 1963. The Chieftain finally entered service with the British Army only in 1967 as there were problems with the engine, transmission and suspension. The Chieftain has now replaced the Centurion gun tank in the British Army. Total production for the British Army amounted to 700 or 800 tanks. In 1971 the Iranian Army placed an order for 700 Chieftains, this order being followed by a further order for a new model called the Shir Iran. In 1976 Kuwait placed an order for about 130 Chieftains. The Chieftain has a hull front of cast construction, with the rest of the hull of welded construction, and the turret is of all cast construction. The driver is seated in the front of the hull in the semi-reclined position, a feature which has enabled the overall height of the hull to be kept to a minimum. The commander and gunner are on the

Right: Chieftain MBT Mk5 with thermal sleeve for 120mm gun. All front line Chieftains of the British Army are now being fitted with the Marconi Space and Defence Systems Integrated Fire Control System which gives the tank an increased hit probability.

Above: Chieftain negotiating rough ground. In addition to being used by the British Army it is also used by Iran and Kuwait.

right of the turret, with the loader on the left. The commander's cupola can be traversed independently of the main turret by hand. The engine and transmission are at the rear of the hull. Suspension is of the Horstmann type, and consists of six road wheels, with the idler at the front and the drive sprocket at the rear, and there are three track-return rollers. The main armament consists of a 120mm gun with an elevation of +20° and a depression of −10°, traverse being 360°. A GEC-Marconi stabilisation system is fitted, enabling the gun to be fired whilst the tank is moving across country with a good chance of a first-round hit. A 7.62mm machine-gun is mounted co-axially with the main armament and there is a similar weapon in the commander's cupola, aimed and fired from within the cupola. When originally introduced the gunner aimed the 120mm gun using a .5in ranging machine gun, but this has now been removed from British Chieftains and the gunner now uses the Barr and Stroud laser rangefinder to obtain correct range to the target. A six-barrelled smoke discharger is mounted on each side of the turret. Some 64 rounds of 120mm and 6,000 rounds of 7.62mm ammunition are carried (Chieftain Mk 5 only). The 120mm gun fires a variety of ammuni- ▶

Main armament of the Chieftain MBT consists of a 120mm rifled tank gun designed by the Royal Armament Research and Development Establishment at Fort Halstead. This fires a wide range of separate loading ammunition (eg, projectile and bagged charge) including Armour Piercing Discarding Sabot Tracer (APDS-T), High Explosive Squash Head (HESH) and Smoke, plus training rounds.

tion, of the separate-loading type, including High-Explosive Squash Head (HESH), Armour-Piercing Discarding Sabot (APDS), Smoke, Canister and Practice. The separate-loading ammunition (separate projectile and charge) makes the job of loader a lot easier, and also enables the projectiles and charges to be stowed separately, which is considerably safer. When the HESH round hits the target, it is compressed on to the armour, so that when the charge explodes shock waves cause the inner surface of the armour to fracture and break up, pieces of the armour then flaking off and flying round the fighting compartment. The APDS round consists of a sub-calibre projectile with a sabot (a light, sectioned 'sleeve' that fits round the projectile and fills the full bore of the gun) around it: when the round leaves the barrel of the gun the sabot splits up and falls off, the projectile then travelling at a very high velocity until it strikes the target and pushes its way through the armour. The Chieftain is fitted with a full range of night-vision equipment including an infra-red searchlight, mounted on the left side of the turret. An NBC pack is fitted in the rear of the turret. This takes in contaminated air, which is then passed through filters before it enters the fighting compartment as clean air. The Chieftain can ford streams to a depth of 3ft 6in (1.066m) without preparation. Deep fording kits have been developed but are not standard issue. The Chieftain can be fitted with an hydraulically operated dozer blade if required. There are two special variants of the Chieftain, the FV4204 Armoured Recovery Vehicle and the FV4205 Bridgelayer. The latter was the first model to enter service and is built at the Royal Ordnance Factory at Leeds. This has a crew of three and weighs just over 53 tons (53,851kg). Two types of bridge can be fitted: the No 8 bridge to span ditches up to 74ft 10in (22.8m) in width, and the No 9 bridge to

span gaps of up to 40ft (12.2m). The bridgelayer takes three to five minutes to lay the bridge and 10 minutes to recover it. The Chieftain ARV has now replaced the Centurion ARV. The vehicle has a crew of four and a combat weight of 52 tons (52,835kg). Two winches are fitted, one with a capacity of 30 tons (30,482kg) and the other with a capacity of 3 tons (3,048kg). When the spade at the front of the vehicle is lowered, the main winch has a maximum capacity of 90 tons (91,445kg). Armament consists of a cupola-mounted 7.62mm machine-gun and smoke dischargers.

In 1974 Iran ordered 125 Shir 1s and 1225 Shir 2s. The Shir 1, which was already in production at the time of the collapse of the Shah's regime, is basically the Chieftain Mk5/5(P) with a new powerpack consisting of a Rolls-Royce CV12 TCA 12 cylinder 1200hp diesel, David Brown TN37 transmission, and an Airscrew Howden cooling system. The Shir 2 has the same powerpack as the Shir 1 but in addition has Chobham armour. By late 1978 six Shir 2s had been built. In 1979 Jordan announced that it would order between 200 and 300 tanks from Britain and it is probable that these will be of the Shir 1 type. To replace the Chieftain in the late 1980s the MBT-80 is being designed at the Fighting Vehicles Research and Development Establishment. This will have a four man crew and be armed with a 120mm rifled tank gun; it will be powered by a Rolls-Royce 1500hp diesel coupled to a David Brown TN38 transmission. It is expected that the first prototype of the MBT-80 will be completed in 1983/84.

Below: Chieftain MBT serving with the British Army of the Rhine being refuelled by an Alvis Stalwart (6x6) High Mobility Load Carrier. To the right of the Stalwart is a FV434 repair vehicle.

Infanterikanonvagn 91 Light Tank/Tank Destroyer

Country of origin: Sweden.
Crew: 4.
Armament: One 90mm gun; one 7.62mm machine gun co-axial with main armament; one 7.62mm anti-aircraft machine gun; 12 smoke dischargers.
Armour: Classified.
Dimensions: Length (with gun forwards) 29ft (8.845m); length (hull) 20ft 1in (6.14m); width 9ft 10in (3m); height 7ft 9in (2.355m).
Weight: (combat) 35,941lbs (15,300kg).
Ground pressure: 0.46kg/cm².
Engine: Volvo-Penta TD 120 A 6-cylinder turbo-charged diesel developing 350hp at 2200 rpm.
Performance: Road speed 43mph (69kmh); range 342 miles (550km); vertical obstacle 2ft 8in (0.8m); trench 9ft 2in (2.8m); gradient 50 per cent.
History: Entered service with Swedish Army in 1975. Still in production.

In the early 1960s Hägglund and Söner were awarded a contract by the Swedish Army Materiel Administration to develop a new full tracked armoured personnel carrier. This became the Pbv 302 and was in production from 1966 to 1971. It was followed in production by the Bärgningsbandvagn 82 armoured recovery vehicle and the Brobandvagn 941 armoured bridge-layer. In 1968 the company was awarded a development contract for a new vehicle to replace the Strv 74 light tank, Ikv-102 and Ikv-103 infantry cannons and the Pansarvarnskanonvagn m/63 self-propelled gun. The first of three prototypes of this vehicle, called the Infanterikanonvagn 91 (or Ikv-91 for short), was completed in 1969; pre-production vehicles were ready in 1974 and the first production model was completed late in 1975.

As in their previous designs, Hägglund have used standard automotive components wherever possible in the vehicle, which have not only enabled costs to be kept to a minimum but also meant that spare parts can be ▶

Above: The Ikv 91 fires its L/54 90mm gun from cover. The low-pressure gun is claimed to create less recoil loads and reduce muzzle effects (flash, smoke, thrown-up dust) than others.

Below: Sweden's Ikv 91, which is designed to operate with anti-tank units in almost any terrain. It has good cross-country performance, and operates well in regions where there is marshy ground and water obstacles, such as rivers and lakes.

Above: In water the Ikv is propelled by its tracks, giving a speed of 7km/h, sufficient to cross moderately fast flowing rivers. For amphibious operation a trim vane is erected and low screens are raised for air inlets and outlets and for the exhaust.

Below: The Ikv 91's low silhouette, well profiled glacis plate and turret front are intended to afford protection, although priority has been given to high mobility.

obtained from normal commercial sources. Some of the components of the Ikv-91 are the same as those used in earlier vehicles developed by the company.

The hull of the Ikv-91 is all of welded steel construction and is divided up into three compartments, driver's at the front, fighting compartment in the centre and engine compartment at the rear. The driver is seated on the left with 18 rounds of ammunition being stowed to his right. The other three members of the crew are seated in the all welded turret with the loader on the left and commander and gunner on the right. The engine compartment is separated from the fighting compartment by a fireproof bulkhead and the engine itself is mounted diagonally to reduce space. The suspension is of the torsion bar type and consists of six large rubber tyred road wheels with the idler at the front and the drive sprocket at the rear. There are no track return rollers and the first and last road wheel stations are provided with a hydraulic shock absorber. The Hägglund-designed tracks can be fitted with studs to give increased traction in snow, but for very deep snow conical spikes, which protrude 50mm below the surface of the link, can be used.

Main armament of the Ikv-91 is a Bofors-designed low pressure gun which fires fin-stabilised high explosive and high explosive anti-tank rounds; a total of 59 rounds of ammunition are carried for the main armament. The main armament has an elevation of $+15°$ and a depression of $-10°$ and the turret can be traversed through a full $360°$; gun elevation and turret traverse are powered with manual controls for emergency use. The gunner's optical sight incorporates a laser rangefinder to give a high probability of a first round hit. A 7.62mm machine gun is mounted co-axial with the main armament and a similar weapon is mounted at the loader's station for use in the anti-aircraft role. Six electrically operated smoke dischargers are mounted either side of the turret.

As there are many lakes in Sweden it was necessary that the Ikv-91 should be fully amphibious. Before entering the water a trim vane is erected at the front of the vehicle (this folds back onto the glacis plate when not in use) and low screens are raised around the air inlets and the exhaust and air outlets and the four bilge pumps switched on. When afloat the Ikv-91 is propelled by its tracks at a maximum speed of 4.34 miles (7kmh). The vehicle is provided with an NBC system but has no night vision equipment at the present time.

Jagdpanzer Kanone/Rakete Tank Destroyer

Jpz. 4-5, Jpz. Rakete
Country of origin: Germany.
Crew: 4.
Armament: One 90mm gun, one 7.62mm MG3 machine-gun co-axial with main armament; one 7.62mm MG3 anti-aircraft machine-gun, eight smoke dischargers.
Armour: 10mm–50mm (0.39–1.96in).
Dimensions: Length (including armament) 28ft 9in (8.75m); length (hull) 20ft 6in (6.238m); width 9ft 9in (2.98m); height (without anti-aircraft machine-gun) 6ft 10in (2.085m).
Weight: Combat 60,627lbs (27,500kg).
Ground pressure: 10.67lb/in² (0.75kg/cm²).
Engine: Daimler-Benz Model MB 837 Aa eight-cylinder water-cooled diesel developing 500hp at 2,200rpm.
Performance: Road speed 43.5mph (70km/h); range 249 miles (400km); vertical obstacle 2ft 6in (0.75m); trench 6ft 7in (2m); gradient 60 per cent.
History: Entered service with the German Army in 1965 and with the Belgian Army in 1975. Production now complete, but see text.

The *Jagdpanzer Kanone* (Jpz.4-5 for short) is a member of a range of vehicles developed for the German Army from the late 1950s, the other two members of the family which reached production being the *Jagdpanzer Rakete* and the *Marder* MICV. The first prototypes were completed in 1960 by Hanomag and Henschel of Germany, and MOWAG of Switzerland. These were followed by further prototypes from the two German companies before the design was finally approved for production. Production began in 1965: 375 were built by Henschel and a similar number by Hanomag, production being completed in 1967. The primary role of the *Jagdpanzer Kanone* is to hunt and destroy enemy tanks. It relies on its low silhouette and speed for its survival — it has a very high road and cross-country speed, and can be driven at the same speed backwards and forwards. The hull of the vehicle is of all-welded steel construction with the maximum armour thickness of 2in (50mm) being concentrated at the front. The fighting

Below: This Jagdpanzer Rakete has one launcher with SS-11 ATGW but is now being rebuilt with HOT ATGW system.

compartment is at the front of the hull, with the engine and transmission at the rear. The suspension is of the torsion-bar type, and consists of five road wheels with the idler at the front and drive sprocket at the rear. There are three track-return rollers on each side. The crew of four consists of the commander, gunner, loader and driver. The 90mm gun is mounted in the front of the hull and is slightly offset to the right. It has a traverse of 15° left and 15° right, and can be elevated from −8° to +15°, both elevation and traverse being manual. A 7.62mm MG3 is mounted co-axially to the right of the main armament, and there is a similar weapon on the commander's hatch for anti-aircraft defence. Eight smoke dischargers are mounted on the roof of the hull, firing forwards. These would be used to cover the withdrawal of the vehicle. The 90mm gun has a maximum effective range of 2,187 yards (2,000m), and a maximum rate of fire of 12 rounds per minute can be achieved. A total of 51 rounds of 90mm and 4,000 rounds of 7.62mm ammunition is carried. An infra-red searchlight is mounted over the main armament, and this moves in elevation and traverse with the gun. The Jpz.4-5 is fitted with an NBC system, and can ford streams to a depth of 4ft 7in (1.4m) without preparation. A wading kit is also available. This can be fitted quickly, and allows the vehicle to ford to a depth ▶

Above: Jagdpanzer Kanone is used both by Belgium (80) and Germany (75) and is armed with a 90mm gun for which 51 rounds of ammunition are carried.

of 6ft 11in (2.1m). The Belgian Army has 80 Jpz.4-5s of a slightly different design, these being assembled in Belgium from components supplied by Germany. The Belgian vehicles use *Marder*-type suspension and a *Marder* transmission, as well as a Belgian-designed fire-control system which incorporates a laser range-finder. The German MG3 machine-guns are replaced by FN MAG 58 weapons of Belgian design and construction. The *Jagdpanzer Rakete* has an almost identical hull to the *Jagdpanzer Kanone* and has been designed to operate with the latter vehicle in order to give long-range anti-tank support. It has two launchers for French SS-11 anti-tank missiles, a total of 14 missiles (minimum range of 547 yards or 500m and maximum range of 3,280 yards or 3,000m) being carried. A total of 370 was built for the German Army between 1967 and 1968. In addition this model has a bow-mounted machine-gun as well as a roof-mounted machine-gun and eight smoke dischargers. Most of the *Jagd-panzer Raketen* are now being refitted with the Euromissile HOT (High-subsonic Optically-guided Tube-launched) missile system. This missile has a number of advantages over the SS-11 missile, including a minimum range of 82 yards (75m), a maximum range of 4,374 yards (4,000m) and simpler loading procedures. It is also much more accurate, and the aimer merely has to keep the target in his sight, which has a magnification of ×7, in order to achieve a hit. For trials purposes a Jagdpanzer has been fitted

with a Hughes TOW ATGW system and it is possible that some of the Jagdpanzer Kanone fleet will be retrofitted with this system to extend their life into the 1980s.

Below: Jagdpanzer Rakete Jaguar 1 armed with HOT ATGW system with missile in ready to launch position; 20 HOTs are carried in all.

Above and left: The 90mm gun of the Jagdpanzer Kanone is mounted in the glacis plate and has a traverse of 15° left and right and can be elevated from −8° to +15°; both traverse and elevation are manual. The vehicles used by the Belgian Army have a more sophisticated fire control system that includes a laser rangefinder.

Leopard 1 Main Battle Tank

Leopard 1, ARV, AEV, AVLB and variants
Country of origin: Germany.
Crew: 4.
Armament: One 105mm gun; one 7.62mm machine-gun co-axial with main armament; one 7.62mm machine-gun on roof; four smoke dischargers on each side of the turret.
Armour: 10mm—70mm (0.39—2.76in).
Dimensions: Length (including main armament) 31ft 4in (9.543m); length (hull) 23ft 3in (7.09m); width 10ft 8in (3.25m); height 8ft 8in (2.64m).
Weight: Combat 88,185lbs (40,000kg).
Ground pressure: 12.23lb/in² (0.86kg/cm²).
Engine: MTU MB 838 Ca.M500 10-cylinder multi-fuel engine developing 830hp at 2,200rpm.
Performance: Road speed 40mph (65km/h); range 373 miles (600km); vertical obstacle 3ft 9in (1.15m); trench 9ft 10in.(3m); gradient 60 per cent.
History: Entered service with the German Army in 1965. In service with Australia, Belgium, Canada, Denmark, Germany, Italy, the Netherlands and Norway.

Without doubt, the Leopard MBT built by Germany has been one of the most successful tanks to be developed since World War II, although when the German Army was re-formed it was equipped with American M47 medium tanks. At one time it was hoped that Germany and France would produce a common tank, but like so many programmes of this type nothing came of it. Prototypes of a new German tank were built by two German consortiums, known as Group A and Group B. At an early stage, however, it was decided to drop the Group B series and continue only with that of Group A. In 1963 it was decided to place this tank in production and the

Below: Leopard 1A3 with infra-red/white searchlight mounted over the 105mm gun that was developed for the Centurion tank.

Above: Early production Leopard 1 MBT of the German Army being recovered by a Leopard armoured recovery vehicle built by MaK.

production contract was awarded to the Krauss-Maffei company of Munich, who are well known for their railway locomotives. The first production Leopard 1 MBT was completed in September 1965 and final deliveries were made by Krauss-Maffei in 1979. Oto Melara in Italy have built 920 Leopard 1s for the Italian Army, bringing Leopard 1 MBT production to 4,561 tanks. The Leopard tank has a crew of four, with the driver in the front of the hull on the right and the other three crew members in the turret. The engine and transmission are at the rear of the hull: the complete Leopard engine can be taken out in well under 30 minutes, which is a great advantage in battle conditions. The main armament of the Leopard is the 105mm L7 series gun manufactured at the Royal Ordnance Factory in Nottingham, ▶

Below: The Leopard 1A3 has a number of improvements including a new all welded steel turret which gives increased protection.

The Leopard 1 at speed. It can reach 40mph (65kph) on made-up roads, a little slower than the Leopard 2.

England. A 7.62mm MG3 machine-gun is mounted co-axially with the main armament and there is a similar machine-gun on the roof of the tank for anti-aircraft defence. Four smoke dischargers are mounted each side of the turret. Sixty rounds of 105mm and 5,500 rounds of machine-gun ammunition are carried. Standard equipment on the Leopard includes night-vision equipment, an NBC system and a crew heater. The vehicle can ford to a maximum depth of 7ft 5in (2.25m) without preparation or 13ft 2in (4m) with the aid of a schnorkel. Since the Leopard entered service it has been constantly updated and the most recent modifications include a stabilisation system for the main armament, thermal sleeve for the gun barrel, new tracks and passive rather than infra-red vision equipment for the driver and commander. Final production model for the German Army was the Leopard 1A4 which has a new all welded turret of spaced armour and integrated fire control system. The Leopard chassis has been the basis for a whole family of variants sharing many common components, some of them (eg the *Gepard*) being manufactured by Krauss-Maffei and others by the

MaK company of Kiel. The first variant to enter service was the Leopard armoured recovery vehicle (ARV). This has been designed to recover disabled vehicles and is fitted with a wide range of equipment including a dozer blade either for dozing operations or for stabilising the vehicle when the crane is being used. The latter is used to change tank engines and other similar components, and can lift a maximum of 19.68 tons (20,000kg). A winch is also provided, and this has a maximum pull of 63.97 tons (65,000kg). The Armoured Engineer Vehicle is almost identical with the ARV, but the dozer can be fitted with special teeth to rip up roadways and an auger is also carried for boring holes in the ground. The bridgelayer model is known as the *Biber* (Beaver); this carries a bridge 72ft 2in (22m) in length, which can be used to span a gap up to 65ft 8in (20m) in width. The *Gepard* anti-aircraft tank is armed with twin 35mm Oerlikon cannon and is in service with Belgium, Germany and the Netherlands, the latter having a Dutch rather than a German radar system. The Germans have fitted the complete turret of the AMX-30 155mm GCT self-propelled gun to a Leopard chassis, but this has yet to be adopted. A driver training model of the Leopard without the gun turret is used by Belgium, Germany and the Netherlands.

Leopard 2 Main Battle Tank

Country of origin: Germany.
Crew: 4.
Armament: One 120mm gun; one 7.62mm MG3 machine-gun co-axial with main armament; one 7.62mm MG anti-aircraft machine-gun; eight smoke dischargers on each side of turret.
Armour: Classified.
Dimensions: Length (including main armament) 31ft 6in (9.61m); length (hull) 24ft 3in (7.4m); width 12ft 3in (3.73m); height 9ft (2.73m).
Weight: Combat 121,275lbs (55,000kg).
Ground pressure: 0.85kg/cm².
Engine: MTU MB 873 Ka-500 12-cylinder water-cooled multi-fuel engine developing 1,500hp at 2,600rpm.
Performance: Road speed 42mph (68km/h); range 310 miles (500km); vertical obstacle 3ft 11in (1.2m); trench 9ft 10in (3m); gradient 60 per cent.
History: First production tanks completed late 1979, entered service with German Army in 1980. On order for Netherlands.

The development of the Leopard 2 MBT can be traced back to a project started in the 1960s. At this time the Germans and the Americans were still working on the MBT-70 programme, so this project had a very low priority. Once the MBT-70 was cancelled in January 1970, the Germans pushed ahead with the Leopard 2, and 17 prototypes were completed by 1974. These prototypes were built by the manufacturers of the Leopard 1, Krauss-Maffei of Munich, with the assistance of many other German companies. Without doubt, the Leopard 2 is one of the most advanced tanks in the world and the Germans have succeeded in designing a tank with high success in all three areas of tank design: mobility, firepower and armour ►

Above: The Leopard 2 shows its paces through mud. In 1977 the German Army ordered 1800; the first was delivered late in 1979 and production will continue through to 1986. MaK of Kiel will produce 810 and Krass-Maffei of Munich the remainder.

Left: Main armament of the Leopard 2 is a 120mm Rhein-Metall smooth-bore gun which fires two types of fixed ammunition, APFSDS (Armour-Piercing Fin-Stabilised Discarding Sabot) and HEAT-MP (High-Explosive Anti-Tank Multi-Purpose). A total of 42 rounds of 120mm ammunition are carried.

A Leopard 2 MBT represents a small, low
target, protruding from cover. In addition
to being ordered by the West German
Army, the Dutch Army has placed an
order for some 445 Leopard 2s, and these
should all be in service by late 1986.

The Leopard 2 has proved itself capable of high mobility over all types of terrain. Its survivability on the battlefields of the 1980s could depend on its high protection and agility.

protection. In the past most tanks have only been able to achieve two of these objectives at once. A good example is the British Chieftain, which has an excellent gun and good armour, but poor mobility; the French AMX-30 is at the other end of the scale and has good mobility, an adequate gun but rather thin armour. The layout of the Leopard 2 is conventional, with the driver at the front, turret with commander, gunner and loader in the centre, and the engine and transmission at the rear. The engine was in fact originally developed for the MBT-70. The complete powerpack can be removed in about 15 minutes for repair or replacement. At first it was widely believed that the Leopard 2's armour was of the spaced type, but late in 1976 it was revealed that it used the British-developed Chobham armour. This gives superior protection against attack from all known projectiles. It is of the laminate type, and consists of layers of steel and ceramics. The suspension system is of the torsion-bar type with dampers. It has seven road wheels, with the drive sprocket at the rear and the idler at the front, and there are four track-return rollers. The first prototypes were armed with a 105mm gun of the smooth-bore type, developed by Rheinmetall, but later prototypes had the 120mm smooth-bore gun. The 120mm gun fires two basic types of fin-stabilised ammunition (in which small fins unfold from the rear of the round just after it has left the barrel), and this means that the barrel does not need to be rifled. The anti-tank round is of the Armour-Piercing Discarding Sabot type, and has an effective range of well over 2,405 yards (2,200m); at this range it will penetrate a standard NATO heavy tank target. The second round is also fin-stabilised and is designed for use against field fortifications and other battlefield targets. The cartridge case is semi-combustible and only the cartridge stub, which is made of conventional

steel, remains after the round has been fired. The job of the loader is eased by the use of the hydraulically-assisted loading mechanism. The gun has an elevation of +20° and a depression of −9°. A standard 7.62mm MG3 machine-gun is mounted co-axially with the main armament. A 7.62mm MG3 machine-gun is installed on the loader's hatch for use in the anti-aircraft role. 42 rounds of 120mm and 2,000 rounds of 7.62mm ammunition are carried. Eight smoke dischargers are mounted each side of the turret, although production vehicles may well have eight on each side. A very advanced fire-control system is fitted, which includes a combined laser and stereoscopic rangefinder, and the gun is fully stabilised, enabling it to be laid and fired on the move with a high probability of the round hitting the target. Standard equipment includes infra-red and passive night-vision equipment, an NBC system and heaters for both the driver's and fighting compartments. The Leopard 2 can ford streams to a depth of 2ft 7in (0.8m) without preparation, and with the aid of a schnorkel can deep ford to a depth of 13ft 1in (4m). In 1976 a modified version of the tank was delivered to the United States for trials. This is designated the Leopard 2 (AV), the letters standing for Austere Version. This has many modifications requested by the United States, including a redesigned turret fitted with the standard 105mm NATO rifled tank gun, a new fire-control system with a Hughes laser rangefinder, modified suspension and so on. It was thought by many that this would have been built in the United States in place of the XM1, but Chrysler won a contract for the latter in November 1976. The West German Army has ordered 1800 Leopard 2 MBT's, of which 990 will be built by Krauss-Maffei of Munich and the remaining 810 by MaK of Kiel. First production tanks were delivered in October 1979 and production will continue until 1986. In 1979 the Netherlands Army placed an order for 445 Leopard 2 MBTs for delivery between 1982 and 1986. Currently at the design stage in West Germany is the Kampfpanzer 3 which will replace the Leopard 1 in the late 1980s.

M41 Walker Bulldog Light Tank

M41, M41A1, M41A2, M41A3
Country of origin: United States of America.
Crew: 4.
Armament: One 76mm gun; one .3in machine-gun co-axial with main armament; one .5in anti-aircraft machine-gun.
Armour: 9.25mm—38mm (0.36—1.49in).
Dimensions: Length (gun forward) 26ft 11in (8.212m); length (hull) 19ft 1in (5.819m); width 10ft 6in (3.198m); height (including .5in machine-gun 10ft 1in (3.075m).
Weight: Combat 51,800lbs (23,495kg).
Ground pressure: 10.24lb/in² (0.72kg/cm²).
Engine: Continental or Lycoming AOS-895-3 6-cylinder petrol engine developing 500bhp at 2,800rpm.
Performance: Road speed 45mph (72km/h); range 100 miles (161km); vertical obstacle 2ft 4in (0.711m); trench 6ft (1.828m); gradient 60 per cent.
History: Entered service with United States Army in 1951. No longer used by the United States but still in service with Argentina, Belgium, Bolivia, Brazil, Chile, Denmark, Ecuador, Ethiopia, Japan, Lebanon, New Zealand, Pakistan, the Philippines, Portugal, Saudi-Arabia, Somalia, Spain, Taiwan, Thailand, Tunisia, Turkey and Vietnam.

The standard light tank in use with the United States Army at the end of World War II was the M24 Chaffee, which weighed 18 tons (18,289kg) and was armed with a 75mm gun. Shortly after the end of the war work started on a new light tank called the T37. The first prototype of this was completed in 1949 and was known as the T37 Phase I. This was followed by the T37 Phase II, which had a redesigned turret and different fire-control system. This model was then redesignated as the T42 and a slightly modified version of this, the T41E1, was standardised as the M41. The M41 was authorised for production in 1949 and was named the Little Bulldog, although the name was subsequently changed to the Walker Bulldog after General W. W. Walker, killed in an accident in Korea in 1951. Production of the M41 was undertaken by the Cadillac Car Division of the General Motors Corporation at the Cleveland Tank Plant, and first production models were completed in 1951. Further models of the M41 were the M41A1, M41A2 and the M41A3. These have a slightly different gun control system, whilst the M41A2 and M41A3 have a fuel-injection system for the engine. The M41 was one of the three main tanks developed for the US Army in the early 1950s, the others being the M47 medium and M103 heavy tanks. The M41 was the first member of a whole family of vehicles sharing many common components. The family included the M42 self-propelled anti-aircraft gun,

Right: The M41 light tank was one of three tanks developed by the United States in the early 1950s, the others being the M47 medium tank and the M103 heavy tank. The M41 shares many common components with the M42 twin 40mm self-propelled anti-aircraft gun and the M44 (155mm) and M52 (105mm) self-propelled howitzers. It was replaced in the United States Army by the M551 Sheridan but large numbers of M41s remain in service with other countries in all parts of the world. Main armament consists of a 76mm M32 gun.

the M44 and M52 self-propelled howitzers and the M75 armoured personnel carrier. In addition there were many trials versions in the 1950s. More recently M42s have been used by the United States Navy. Fitted with remote-control equipment, they are used as mobile targets for new air-to-ground missiles. The hull of the M41 is of all-welded steel construction, whilst the turret is of welded and cast construction. The driver is seated at the front of the hull on the left, with the other three crew members in the turret, the commander and gunner on the right and the loader on the left. The engine and transmission are at the rear of the hull, and are separated from the fighting compartment by a fireproof bulkhead. Like most American AFVs of that period, the M41 is provided with a hull escape hatch, thus enabling the crew to leave the vehicle with a better chance of survival than if they baled out via the turret or driver's hatch. The suspension is of the torsion-bar type and consists of five road wheels, with the drive sprocket at the rear and the idler at the front. There are three track-return rollers. The main armament of the M41 consists of a 76mm gun with an elevation of $+19°$ and a depression of $-9°$, traverse being $360°$. A .3in machine-gun is mounted to the left of the main armament and there is a .5in Browning machine-gun on the commander's cupola. Some 65 rounds of 76mm, 2,175 rounds of .5in and 5,000 rounds of .3in ammunition are carried. The barrel of the 76mm gun is provided with a bore evacuator and a 'T' type blast-deflector, the latter's function being to reduce the effects of blast and obscuration caused by the flow of propellant gases into the atmosphere. These gases otherwise raise a dust cloud and make aiming of the weapon more difficult. When developed the M41 was to have been fitted with an automatic loader (this was the T37 Phase III), but this was not installed in production vehicles. The M41 was also fitted with a 90mm gun for trials purposes, under the designation T49, but this did not progress beyond the prototype stage. The M41 can ford to a maximum depth of 3ft 4in (1.016m) without preparation or 8ft (2.44m) with the aid of a kit. Infra-red driving lights are provided, and some models have an infra-red searchlight for engaging targets at night. The M41 has been replaced by the M551 Sheridan in the United States Army, but is still used by many countries in most parts of the world.

M44 Self-propelled Howitzer

M44, M44A1
Country of origin: United States of America.
Crew: 5.
Armament: One 155mm howitzer; one .5in machine-gun for anti-aircraft use.
Armour: 12.7mm (0.50in) maximum.
Dimensions: Length 20ft 2½in (6.159m); width 10ft 7½in (3.238m); height (overall) 10ft 2½in (3.111m).
Weight: Combat 62,500lbs (28,350kg).
Ground pressure: 9.38lb/in² (0.66kg/cm²).
Engine: Continental AOS-895-3 six-cylinder air-cooled petrol engine developing 500hp at 2,800rpm.
Performance: Road speed 35mph (56km/h); range 76 miles (122km); vertical obstacle 2ft 6in (0.762m); trench 6ft (1.828m); gradient 60 per cent.
History: Entered service with the United States Army in 1952. Still used by Belgium, Greece, Italy, Japan, Jordan, Spain, Turkey and the United States.

In 1947 there started development of a 155mm self-propelled howitzer designated the T99. It was then decided to use some of the components of a new light tank, the T41 (later to become the M41 Walker Bulldog), and with these components the T99 became the T99E1, which was then placed in production. A total of 250 T99E1s was built, but these vehicles had numerous deficiencies. After modification the type was placed in production again under the designation T194, and later the 250 T99E1s were rebuilt to the new standard. In 1953 the T194 was standardised as the M44. This was followed in 1956 by the M44A1, which has a fuel-injection system for the engine. Production of the M44 was undertaken by the Massey Harris company. The 105mm M52 self-propelled howitzer shares many components with the M44, but is no longer used by the United States Army. The M44 has been replaced in the British, German and United States Armies by the 155mm M109 self-propelled howitzer. The hull of the M44 is of all-welded construction with the engine and transmission at the front and the fighting compartment at the rear. The latter has no overhead protection, although steel hoops and a tarpaulin can be fitted if required. The suspension is of the torsion-bar type and consists of six road wheels, with the drive

Below: The M44 is armed with a 155mm M45 howitzer which is mounted in an open topped compartment at the rear of the vehicle and can fire an HE projectile weighing some 42.91kg to a range of 14,600m, and a variety of other ammunition.

Above: The M44 SPH has the same chassis as the M52 SPH and shares many common automotive components with the M41 tank.

sprocket at the front and the sixth road wheel acting as the idler. There are four track-return rollers. A large spade is mounted at the rear of the hull and this is lowered before fire is opened. The 155mm howitzer has an elevation of +65° and a depression of −5°, traverse being 30° left and 30° right. A variety of ammunition can be fired, including High Explosive, Chemical, Nuclear, Smoke and Illuminating. A standard .5in Browning machine-gun is mounted for anti-aircraft defence on the right of the fighting compartment. Some 24 rounds of 155mm and 900 rounds of .5in ammunition are carried. The M44 can ford to a maximum depth of 3ft 6in (1.066m).

Below: Production of the M44 was undertaken by Massey Harris in the mid-1950s. It has now been replaced in the United States Army, and the British and German armies, by the 155mm M109 but remains in service with a few countries.

M47 Medium Tank

M47, M102
Country of origin: United States of America.
Crew: 5.
Armament: One 90mm M36 gun; one .3in M1919A4E1 machine-gun in bow; one .3in M1919A4E1 machine-gun co-axial with main armament; one .5in M2 machine-gun on commander's cupola.
Armour: 12.7mm—115mm (0.50in—4.60in).
Dimensions: Length (gun forward) 28ft 1in (8.508m); length (hull) 20ft 8in (6.307m); width 10ft 6in (3.51m); height (including anti-aircraft machine-gun) 11ft (3.352m).
Weight: Combat 101,775lbs (46,170kg).
Ground pressure: 13.3lb/in² (0.935kg/cm²).
Engine: Continental AV-1790-5B 12-cylinder air-cooled petrol engine developing 810bhp at 2,800rpm.
Performance: Road speed, 30mph (48km/h); range 80 miles (130km); vertical obstacle 3ft (0.914m); trench 8ft 6in (2.59m); gradient 60 per cent.
History: Entered service with the United States Army in 1952. Still used by Austria, Belgium, Brazil, Greece, Iran, Italy, Jordan, Pakistan, Portugal, South Korea, Spain, Taiwan, Turkey and Yugoslavia. The M47 is no longer used by France, Germany or the United States.

After the end of World War II the M26 Pershing heavy tank was reclassified as a medium tank, and further development of the type resulted in the M46 medium tank. The M46 and M26 were the standard US medium tanks when the Korean War broke out in 1950. A new medium tank, the T42, was being developed, but this was not yet ready for production. To meet the urgent need to get an improved medium tank into production, a modified M26 tank chassis was fitted with the turret of the new T42 tank, armed with a new 90mm gun. This then became the M47 medium tank, also known as the Patton 1. Production started almost immediately at the Detroit Tank Arsenal and the American Locomotive Company, but the M47 did not see

Below: The M47 was developed during the Korean War and is essentially a modified M26 Pershing chassis fitted with the turret developed for the T42 tank. Over 8500 M47s were completed in the 1950s.

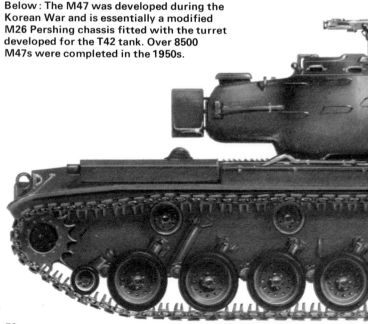

combat in Korea. The hull and the turret of the M47 are of all-cast construction. The driver is seated at the front of the hull on the left with the bow machine-gunner to his right. The commander and gunner are on the right of the turret, with the loader on the left. The engine and transmission are at the rear of the hull. The suspension is of the torsion-bar type and consists of six road wheels, with the drive sprocket at the rear and the idler at the front. There are three track-return rollers and a small tensioning wheel is located between the last road wheel and the drive sprocket. (When a tank is new its tracks tend to be fairly tight, but as these wear in service the tensioning wheel then takes up some of the slack.) The M47 has 86 track shoes per track when delivered. The main armament of the M47 consists of a 90mm gun with an elevation of +19° and a depression of −5°, traverse being 360° ▶

Above: Austrian Army M47 moves up with infantry support. The M47 was soon replaced in the US Army by the much improved M48 but large numbers of these tanks are still in service in most parts of the world. The M47 was the last American tank to have a bow mounted MG.

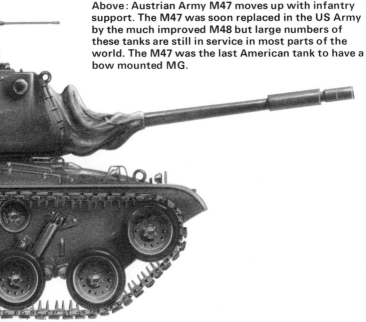

Elevation and traverse are powered, although manual controls for use in an emergency are provided. A .3in machine-gun is mounted co-axially to the left of the main armament, and there is a similar weapon in the bow. The M47 was the last American tank to have a bow-mounted machine-gun. These have been dispensed with as they make an additional crew member necessary, and this space can be better used to carry additional fuel and ammunition. Some 71 rounds of 90mm, 440 rounds of .5in and 4,125 rounds of .3in ammunition are carried. The M47 has infra-red driving lights but no NBC system. The tank can ford streams to a maximum depth of 4ft (1.219m) without preparation. A special amphibious kit, designated T15, was developed for the M47; but this was not adopted. This kit consisted of large pontoons attached to the sides, front and rear of the hull, and the tank was propelled in the water by two propellers. As the M47 was replaced a few years after it entered service by the M48, few variants of the basic type were developed. The M102 was a special model developed for use by the engineers. This had its 90mm gun replaced by a short-barrelled 105mm howitzer. A dozer blade was mounted at the front of the hull and there was a

jib for lifting purposes at the front and rear. A flame-thrower model called the T66 was developed, but this did not enter service. In the 1950s the M47 was issued to many NATO countries under the Military Assistance Program, and some of these still remain in service today. A number of countries, including Austria, France, Italy and Spain, have at various times rebuilt M47s to bring them up to modern standards. For example, in Italy Oto Melara rebuilt an M47 with a new engine and transmission, plus a new electrical system, and replaced the 90mm gun with the standard 105mm British L7 series weapon. This has been offered to a number of armies but has not so far been adopted. The Spanish Army is currently refitting some of its M47s with a new diesel engine and a modified transmission, and numerous other improvements have been incorporated. The M47 was soon replaced in the US Army by the M48, which is a direct development of the earlier M47. Although the M47 was designed almost 30 years ago, it will remain in service with some countries until the 1990s at least. Although under-gunned by today's standards, it is still a reliable and useful vehicle, despite the fact that it has an overly complicated fire-control system.

Right: Head-on view of M47 clearly showing the bow mounted machine gun.

Left and below: The M47 in Turkish Army service. It was supplied to many countries under the US Mutual Aid Program in the 1950s. France, West Germany, Italy and Spain were among the largest users and even today the tank is in service with some NATO countries.

M48 Medium Tank

M48, M48C, M48A1, M48A2, M48A2C, M48A3, M48A4, M48A5, M67, M67A1, M67A2, M48AVLB

Country of origin: United States of America.
Crew: 4.
Armament: One 90mm gun M41; one 0.3in M1919A-4E1 machine-gun co-axial with the main armament (some have a 7.62mm M73 MG); one 0.5in machine-gun in commander's cupola.
Armour: 12.7mm–120mm (0.50–4.80in).
Dimensions: Length (including main armament) 24ft 5in (7.442m); length (hull) 22ft 7in (6.882m); width 11ft 11in (3.631m); height (including cupola) 10ft 3in (3.124m).
Weight: Combat 104,000lbs (47,173kg).
Ground pressure: 11.80lb/in² (0.83kg/cm²).
Engine: Continental AVDS-1790-2A 12-cylinder air-cooled diesel developing 750hp at 2,400rpm.
Performance: Road speed 30mph (48km/h); range 288 miles (463km); vertical obstacle 3ft (0.915m); trench 8ft 6in (2.59m); gradient 60 per cent.
History: Entered service with the United States Army in 1953. Used by Germany, Greece, Iran, Israel, Jordan, Morocco, Norway, Pakistan, South Korea, Spain, Taiwan, Thailand, Turkey, United States and Vietnam.

Once the M47 was authorized for production, development started on a new medium tank as the M47 was only a stop-gap measure. So in October 1950 Detroit Arsenal started design work on a new medium tank armed with a 90mm gun. This design study was completed two months later and in December 1950 Chrysler was given a contract to complete the design work and build six prototypes under the designation T48. The first of these prototypes had to be completed by December 1951. Production started in

Right: The M48A5 is an earlier M48 with many improvements including a 105mm gun. It is used mainly by the US National Guard although there are two M48A5 battalions in South Korea.

Above: M67A1 flamethrower tank in action in Vietnam. All US flamethrower tanks have been placed in storage for wartime use.

1952 and first deliveries were made to the US Army the following year. The M48, as it was now called, was followed in production by the M60, essentially an M48A3 with a 105mm gun and other detailed changes, production of this model being undertaken at the Detroit Tank Plant.

The hull of the M48 is of cast armour construction, as is the turret. The driver is seated at the front of the hull with the other three crew members located in the turret, with the commander and gunner on the right and the loader on the left. The engine and transmission are at the rear of the hull, and are separated from the fighting compartment by a fireproof bulkhead. The suspension is of the torsion-bar type and consists of six road wheels, with the drive sprocket at the rear and the idler at the front. Depending on the model there are between three and five track-return rollers, and some models have a small track tensioning wheel between the sixth road wheel and the drive sprocket. The main armament consists of a 90mm gun with an elevation of +19° and a depression of −9°, traverse being 360°. A 0.3in ▶

M1919A4E1 machine-gun is mounted co-axially with the main armament, although most M48s in US Army Service have a 7.62mm M73 machine-gun. There is also a 0.5in MZ machine-gun in the commander's cupola (except on the M48A1 which has a simple mount). This cupola can be traversed through 360°, and the machine-gun can be elevated from −10° to +60°.

The M48 can be fitted with a dozer blade, if required, at the front of the hull. All M48s have infra-red driving lights and some an infra-red/white searchlight mounted over the main armament. The type can ford to a depth of 4ft (1.219m) without preparation or 8ft (2.438m) with the aid of a kit.

The first model to enter service was the M48, and this has a simple cupola for the commander, with the machine-gun mounted externally. The second

Below: M48 of the Israeli Army fitted with 105mm gun. This is also fitted to Israeli Centurion, M60, M60A1 and more recent Merkava MBTs.

model was the M48C, which was for training use only as it has a mild steel hull. The M48A1 was followed by the M48A2, which has many improvements including a fuel-injection system for the engine and larger capacity fuel tanks. The M48A2C was a slightly modified M48A2. The M48A3 was a significant improvement as this has a diesel engine, which increases the vehicle's operational range considerably, and a number of other modifications including a different fire-control system. Latest model is the M48A5, essentially an M48A1, or M48A2 with modifications including a new 105mm gun, new tracks, a 7.62mm M60D co-axial machine-gun and a similar weapon on the loader's hatch, plus many other detail modifications. Three flamethrower tanks were developed: the M67 (using an M48A1 chassis), the M67A1 (using an M48A2 chassis) and the M67A2 (using an M48A3 chassis). Also in service is an M48 Armoured Vehicle-Launched Bridge. This has a scissors bridge which can be laid over gaps up to 60ft (18.288m) in width.

M52 105mm
Self-propelled Howitzer

Country of origin: United States of America.
Crew: 5.
Armament: One 155mm howitzer; one 12.7mm anti-aircraft machine-gun.
Armour: 0.5in (12.7mm).
Dimensions: Length 19ft (5.8m); width 10ft 4in (3.149m); height (includ-ing AA MG) 10ft 10in (3.316m).
Weight: (combat) 53,008lbs (24,040kg).
Ground pressure: 0.6kg/cm^2.
Engine: Continental AOS-895-3 6 cylinder petrol developing 500bhp at 2800rpm.
Performance: Road speed 35mph (56.3kmh); road range 99 miles (160km); vertical obstacle 3ft (0.914m); trench 6ft (1.828m); gradient 60 per cent.
History: Entered service with United States Army in 1955. In service with Greece, Japan, Jordan. Production complete.

In 1946 design studies started at Detroit Arsenal on a new 105mm howitzer carriage to replace wartime models then in use. In 1955 a prototype, the T98E1, was standardised as the Howitzer, Self-Propelled, Full-Tracked, 105mm, M52. The following year the M52A1 was standardised. This is almost identical to the M52 but has a fuel injection engine which gives the vehicle a slightly better range and a maximum road speed of 42mph (67.5kmh) compared to the 35mph (56.3kmh) of the original M52. The M52 and M52A1 were only in front line service with the United States Army for a short period and were replaced from 1962 by the former 105mm M108 self-propelled howitzer which uses the same chassis as the M109.

The hull of the M52 is of all welded steel construction with the engine and transmission at the front of the hull and the turret mounted on the top of the hull at the rear. The suspension is of the torsion bar type and consists of six dual rubber tyred road wheels with the drive sprocket at the front, sixth road wheel acting as the idler and four track return rollers; the first, second, fourth and fifth road wheels have hydraulic shock absorbers.

The five man crew, consisting of the commander, gunner, two loaders and the driver, are all seated in the fully enclosed turret which can be manually

traversed 60° left and 60° right. The 105mm howitzer is elevated manually and has an elevation of +65° and a depression of −10° and can fire a wide range of ammunition including HE, illuminating and smoke to a maximum range of 12,329 yards (11,270m). A total of 102 rounds of 105mm ammunition are carried, some in the turret for ready use, including 21 on a circular vertically positioned drum known as the lazy susan, and the remainder under the turret at the rear of the hull. Access to the latter is via two doors in the rear of the hull. Mounted externally on the turret roof is a standard 12.7mm machine gun for use in the anti-aircraft role; this has an elevation of +85° and a depression of −15°; no protection is provided for the gunner.

The M52 can ford to a depth of 4ft (1.219m) and standard equipment includes a fire extinguishing system, heater, turret ventilator to remove fumes from the turret, and infra-red driving lights; it does not have an NBC system. The chassis of the M52 is almost identical to that of the M44 155mm self-propelled howitzer, but the latter can easily be distinguished from the M52 as the 155mm howitzer is mounted in an open topped compartment at the rear of the hull rather than in a fully enclosed turret.

Above: The M52 105mm SPH has the same chassis as the M44 155mm SPH and shares many automotive components with the M41 Walker Bulldog light tank. It was developed after World War II and entered service in the early 1950s.

Left: M52 105mm SPH of the Japanese Ground Self Defence Forces who acquired 30 of these from the United States in 1965. It is also used by Greece and Jordan.

M60 Main Battle Tank

M60, M60A1, M60A2, M60A3, M60 AVLB, M728 CEV
Country of origin: United States of America.
Crew: 4.
Armament: One 105mm gun; one 7.62mm machine-gun co-axial with main armament; one 0.5in anti-aircraft machine-gun in commander's cupola.
Armour: 12.7mm—120mm (0.50—4.80in).
Dimensions: Length (gun forward) 30ft 6in (9.309m); length (hull) 22ft 9½in (6.946m); width 11ft 11in (3.631m); height 10ft 8in (3.257m).
Weight: Combat 108,000lbs (48,987kg).
Ground pressure: 11.24lb/in² (0.79kg/cm²).
Engine: Continental AVDS-1790-2A 12-cylinder diesel developing 750bhp at 2,400rpm.
Performance: Road speed 30mph (48km/h); range 310 miles (500km); vertical obstacle 3ft (0.914m); trench 8ft 6in (2.59m); gradient 60 per cent.
History: The M60 entered service with the United States Army in 1960 and is also used by Austria, Ethiopia, Iran, Israel, Italy, Jordan, North Yemen, Saudi Arabia, Singapore, Somalia, South Korea, Sudan, Turkey and the United States Marine Corps.

In the 1950s the standard tank of the United States Army was the M48. In 1957 an M48 series tank was fitted with a new engine for trials purposes and this was followed by another three prototypes in 1958. Late in 1958 it was decided to arm the new tank with the British 105mm L7 series gun, to be built in the United States under the designation M68. In 1959 the first production order for the new tank, now called the M60, was placed with Chrysler, and the type entered production at Detroit Tank Arsenal in late 1959, with the first production tanks being completed the following year.

From late in 1962, the M60 was replaced in production by the M60A1, which has a number of improvements, the most important being the

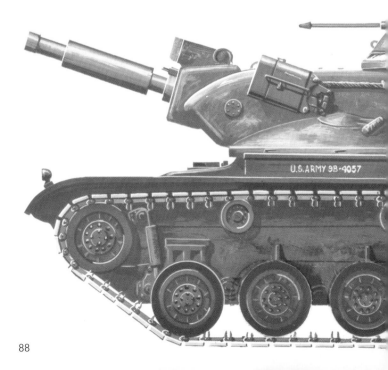

redesigned turret. The M60A1 has a turret and hull of all-cast construction. The driver is seated at the front of the hull with the other three crew members in the turret, commander and gunner on the right and the loader on the left. The engine and transmission are at the rear, the latter having one reverse and two forward ranges. The M60 has torsion-bar suspension and six road wheels, with the idler at the front and the drive sprocket at the rear; there are four track-return rollers. The 105mm gun has an elevation of +20° and a depression of −10°, and traverse is 360°. Both elevation and traverse are powered. A 7.62mm M73 machine-gun is mounted co-axially with the main ▶

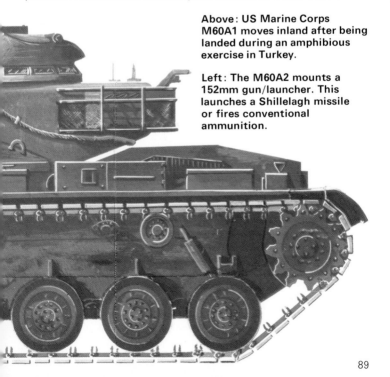

Above: US Marine Corps M60A1 moves inland after being landed during an amphibious exercise in Turkey.

Left: The M60A2 mounts a 152mm gun/launcher. This launches a Shillelagh missile or fires conventional ammunition.

armament and there is a 0.5in M85 machine-gun in the commander's cupola. The latter can be aimed and fired from within the turret, and has an elevation of +60° and a depression of −15°. Some 60 rounds of 105mm, 900 rounds of 0.5in and 5,950 rounds of 7.62mm ammunition are carried. Infra-red driving lights are fitted as standard and an infra-red/white light is mounted over the main armament. All M60s have an NBC system. The tank can also be fitted with a dozer blade on the front of the hull. The M60 can ford to a depth of 4ft (1.219m) without preparation or 8ft (2.438m) with the aid of a kit. For deep fording operations a schnorkel can be fitted, allowing the M60 to ford to a depth of 13ft 6in (4.114m). The M60A2 was developed in 1964–65 and consists of an M60 chassis with a new turret armed with the 152mm gun/launcher, which can fire a variety of ammunition with a combustible cartridge case or a Shillelagh missile. The M60A2 entered production in 1966, but it was not until 1974 that the first M60A2 unit was formed as many problems were encountered with the whole Shillelagh/M60A2/Sheridan programme. The M60A2 is used only by the United States Army and just over 500 were built. The M60A2 also has a 7.62mm co-axial machine-gun and a 0.5in M85 anti-aircraft machine-gun. Thirteen Shillelagh

Below: M60A1 of the US Marine Corps. Production of the latest model, the M60A3, will continue at Detroit until the early 1980s.

Above: M60A2 MBTs during a night firing exercise. The tank is armed with a 152mm gun/launcher which can fire a variety of conventional types of ammunition or the Ford Shillelagh missile.

missiles, and 33 rounds of conventional 152mm, 5,560 rounds of 7.62mm and 1,080 rounds of 0.5in ammunition are carried. A major improvement program for the M60A1 is currently under way, and this is scheduled to be completed in a few years' time. Tanks built with these modifications are known as the M60A3. Not all of these modifications have been cleared for production yet, but the full list of improvements is as follows: a stabilization system for the main armament, a laser rangefinder which is being developed by Hughes, new night-vision equipment, an improved engine and air cleaners, new tracks, a modified cupola and a thermal sleeve for the main armament. There are two other variants of the M60 series, the M728 Combat Engineer Vehicle and the M60 Armoured Vehicle-Launched Bridge.

Production of the M60 series of MBTs now exceeds 6,000 and production is expected to continue at the Detroit Tank Plant to 1981/82, after which time the plant will tool up for production of the XM1 (M1).

Below: A total of 526 M60A2s were built at Detroit in the 1960s but due to many problems the tank did not enter service until 1975.

M107 Self-propelled Gun/ M110 Self-propelled Howitzer

M107, M110, M110A, M110A2
Crew: 5.
Country of origin: United States of America.
Armament: One 175mm gun.
Dimensions: Length (including gun and spade in travelling position) 36ft 11in (11.256m); length (hull) 18ft 9in (5.72m); width 10ft 4in (3.149m); height (to top of barrel in travelling position) 12ft 1in (3.679m).
Weight: Combat 62,098lbs (28,168kg).
Ground pressure: 11.52lb/in^2 (0.81kg/cm^2).
Engine: Detroit Diesel Model 8V71T eight-cylinder turbocharged diesel developing 405hp at 2,300rpm.
Performance: Road speed 35mph (56km/h); range 450 miles (725km); vertical obstacle 3ft 4in (1.016m); trench 7ft 9in (2.362m); gradient 60 per cent.
Armour: 20mm (0.79in) maximum, estimated..
History: Entered service with the United States Army in 1963. Also used by Britain, Germany, Greece, Iran, Israel, Italy, the Netherlands, South Korea, Spain, and Turkey.

Above: The hydraulically operated spade at the rear of the M110 is lowered before firing commences to provide a stable base.

In 1956 the United States Army issued a requirement for a range of self-propelled artillery which would be air-transportable. The Pacific Car and Foundry Company of Washington were awarded the development contract and from 1958 built three different self-propelled weapons on the same chassis. These were the T235 (175mm gun), which became the M107, the T236 (203mm howitzer), which became the M110, and the T245 (155mm gun), which was subsequently dropped from the range. These prototypes were powered by a petrol engine, but it was soon decided to replace this by a diesel engine as this could give the vehicles a much greater range of action. When fitted with a diesel engine the T235 became the T235E1 and after further trials this was placed in production as the M107 in 1962, entering service with the army the following year. The M107 has in fact been built by three different companies at various times: FMC, Bowen-McLaughlin York and the Pacific Car and Foundry Company. It is not currently in production. The hull is of all-welded aluminium construction with the driver at the front on the left with the engine to his right. The gun

Above: M107 175mm gun in action during the Vietnam War firing an HE projectile weighing 66.78kg to a maximum range of 32,800m.

is mounted towards the rear of the hull. The suspension is of the torsion-bar type and consists of five road wheels, with the fifth road wheel acting as the idler; the drive sprocket is at the front. Five crew are carried on the gun (driver, commander and three gun crew), the other eight crew members following in an M548 tracked vehicle (this is based on the M113 APC chassis), which also carries the ammunition, as only two ready rounds are carried on the M107 itself. The 175mm gun has an elevation of +65° and a depression of −2°, traverse being 30° left and 30° right. Elevation and traverse are both powered, although there are manual controls for use in an emergency. The M107 fires an HE round to a maximum range of 35,870 yards (32,800m). A large hydraulically-operated spade is mounted at the rear of the hull and is lowered into position before the gun opens fire, and the suspension can also be locked when the gun is fired to provide a more stable firing platform. The gun can officially fire one round per minute, but a well trained crew can fire at least two rounds a minute. As the projectile is very heavy, an hydraulic hoist is provided to position the projectile on the ▶

ramming tray; the round is then pushed into the breech hydraulically before the charge is pushed home, the breechlock closed and the weapon is then fired. The M107 can ford streams to a maximum depth of 3ft 6in (1.066m) but has no amphibious capability. Infra-red driving lights are fitted as standard but the type does not have an NBC system.

The M110 8in (203mm) self-propelled howitzer has an identical hull and mount as the 175mm M107, and the 8in howitzer has the same elevation and traverse as the 175mm gun. The M110 is easily distinguishable from the M107 as the former has a much shorter and fatter barrel. The howitzer can fire both HE and tactical nuclear rounds to a maximum range of 18,372 yards (16,800m). Both the M110 and the M107 are now being replaced in service with the United States Army and Marines by the M110A1 and M110A2 which have a longer barrel than the standard M110 and are able to fire a variety of ammunition including HE, improved conventional munitions, chemical, dual-purpose, nuclear and rocket-assisted projectiles to a maximum range of 22,966 yards (21,000m), although the rocket-assisted projectiles will have a longer range than this. It has been estimated by the US Army that the total cost to convert all M107s and M110s to the new standard will be about $40,000,000, a great deal less than the cost of building a new vehicle. The M107/M110 is normally fielded in battalions of 12 guns. One of the problems with heavy artillery of this type is keeping the guns supplied with sufficient ammunition. As noted above the weapon is supported by an M548 tracked vehicle, and this in turn is kept supplied by 5- or 10-ton trucks. Another problem is that the M107 has a very high muzzle velocity which means that its barrel, like tank barrels, wears out

Above: M110 of the British Royal Artillery shortly after being fired at the Royal School of Artillery, Larkhill, Wiltshire.

after about 400 rounds have been fired. It takes about two hours to change the barrel on the M107 and spare barrels are held in reserve for just this purpose.

Above: 175mm M107 opens fire in Vietnam. This is now being withdrawn from service in American units and replaced by the much-improved M110A1 and M110A2.

Left: The M110 is also being replaced in the US Army and Marines by the M110A1 and M110A2, capable of firing nuclear rounds.

M109 Self-propelled Howitzer

M109, M109A1, M109A2 and variants
Country of origin: United States of America.
Crew: 6.
Armament: One 155mm howitzer; one .5in (12.7mm) Browning anti-aircraft machine-gun.
Armour: 20mm (0.79in) maximum, estimated.
Dimensions: Length (including armament) 21ft 8in (6.612m); length (hull) 20ft 6in (6.256m); width 10ft 10in (3.295m); height (including anti-aircraft machine-gun) 10ft 9in (3.28m).
Weight: Combat 52,438lbs (23,786kg).
Ground pressure: 10.95lb/in^2 (0.77kg/cm^2).
Engine: Detroit Diesel Model 8V71T eight-cylinder turbocharged diesel developing 405bhp at 2,300rpm.
Performance: Road speed 35mph (56km/h); range 242 miles (390km); vertical obstacle 1ft 9in (0.533m); trench 6ft (1.828m); gradient 60 per cent.
History: Entered service with the United States Army in 1963. Also used by Austria, Belgium, Canada, Denmark, Ethiopia, Germany, Great Britain, Iran, Israel, Italy, Jordan, Libya, Morocco, the Netherlands, Norway, Pakistan, Spain, Switzerland, Turkey and Vietnam.

The first production models of the M109 were completed in 1962, and some 4,000 examples have now been built, making the M109 the most widely used self-propelled howitzer in the world. It has a hull of all-welded aluminium construction, providing the crew with protection from small arms fire. The driver is seated at the front of the hull on the left, with the engine to his right. The other five crew members are the commander, gunner and three ammunition members, all located in the turret at the rear of the hull. There

Below: M109A1 firing a Martin Marietta Copperhead Cannon Launched Guided Projectile (CLGP) at White Sands Missile Range, USA.

Above: 155mm M109 self-propelled howitzer at a fire support base at Phu Bai in Vietnam. Well over 3,000 M109s have now been built.

is a large door in the rear of the hull for ammunition resupply purposes. Hatches are also provided in the sides and rear of the turret. There are two hatches in the roof of the turret, the commander's hatch being on the right. A 0.5in (12.7mm) Browning machine-gun is mounted on this for anti-aircraft defense. The suspension is of the torsion-bar type and consists of ▶

Below: The combat weight of the M109 has been kept to under 24 tonnes by extensive use of aluminium in its construction.

Above: Prototype of the M109A1 was the M109A1E1 shown here at Aberdeen Proving Ground. It fires a 42.91kg HE projectile to a range of 18,100m compared to 14,600m in the original M109.

seven road wheels, with the drive sprocket at the front and the idler at the rear, and there are no track-return rollers.

The 155mm howitzer has an elevation of +75° and a depression of –3°, and the turret can be traversed through 360°. Elevation and traverse are powered, with manual controls for emergency use. The weapon can fire a variety of ammunition, including HE, tactical nuclear, illuminating, smoke and chemical rounds. A total of 28 rounds of separate-loading ammunition is carried, as well as 500 rounds of machine-gun ammunition. The second model to be introduced was the M109A1, identical with the M109 apart from its much longer barrel, which is provided with a fume extractor as well as a muzzle-brake. The fume extractor removes propellent gases from the barrel after a round has been fired and thus prevents fumes from entering the fighting compartment. The M109 fires a round to a maximum range of 16,076 yards (14,700m), whilst the M109A1 fires to a maximum range of 19,685 yards (18,000m). The M109 can ford streams to a maximum depth of 5ft (1.828m). A special amphibious kit has been developed for the vehicle but this is not widely used. It consists of nine inflatable airbags, normally carried by a truck. Four of these are fitted to each side of the hull and the last to the front of the hull. The vehicle is then propelled in the water by its tracks at a maximum speed of 4mph (6.4km/h). The M109 is provided with infra-red driving lights and some vehicles also have an NBC system.

Right: M109A1 of the 7th United States Army based in Europe. It is deployed in battalions consisting of three batteries, each having six guns that can fire a tactical nuclear projectile.

99

M551 Sheridan Light Tank

Country of origin: United States of America.
Crew: 4.
Armament: One 152mm gun/missile launcher; one 7.62mm machine-gun co-axial with main armament; one 0.5in anti-aircraft machine-gun; four smoke dischargers on each side of turret.
Armour: Classified.
Dimensions: Length 20ft 8in (6.299m); width 9ft 3in (2.819m); height (overall) 9ft 8in (2.946m).
Weight: Combat 34,898lbs (15,830kg).
Ground pressure: 6.96lb/in^2 (0.49kg/cm^2).
Engine: Detroit Diesel 6V53T six-cylinder diesel developing 300bhp at 2,800rpm.
Performance: Road speed 45mph (70km/h); water speed 3.6mph (5.8km/h); range 373 miles (600km); vertical obstacle 2ft 9in (0.838m); trench 8ft 4in (2.54m); gradient 60 per cent.
History: Entered service with United States Army in 1966 and still in service.

In August 1959 the United States Army established a requirement for a "new armoured vehicle with increased capabilities over any other weapon in its own inventory and that of any adversary". The following year the Allison Division of General Motors was awarded a contract to design a vehicle called the Armored Reconnaissance Airborne Assault Vehicle (ARAAV) to meet the requirement. The first prototype, designated XM551, was completed in 1962, and this was followed by a further 11 prototypes. Late in 1965 a production contract was awarded to Allison, and the first production vehicles were completed in 1966, these being known as the M551 or Sheridan. Production was completed in 1970 after 1,700 vehicles had been built.

The hull of the Sheridan is of all-aluminium construction whilst the turret is of welded steel. The driver is seated at the front of the hull and the other three crew members are in the turret, with the loader on the left and

the gunner and commander on the right. The engine and transmission are at the rear of the hull. The suspension is of the torsion-bar type and consists of five road wheels, with the drive sprocket at the rear and the idler at the front. There are no track-return rollers. The most interesting feature of the Sheridan is its armament system. This consists of a 152mm gun/launcher which has an elevation of +19° and a depression of −8°, traverse being 360°. A 7.62mm machine-gun is mounted co-axially with the main armament, and there is a 0.5in Browning machine-gun on the commander's cupola. The latter cannot be aimed and fired from within the turret, and as a result of combat experience in Vietnam many vehicles have now been fitted with a shield for this weapon. The 152mm gun/launcher, a version of which was fitted to the M60A2 and MBT-70, fires a Shillelagh missile or a variety of conventional ammunition including HEAT-T-MP, WP and canister, all of them having a combustible cartridge case. The Shillelagh missile was developed by the United States Army Missile Command and the Philco-Ford Corporation, and has a maximum range of about 3,281 yards (3,000m). The missile is controlled by the gunner, who simply has to keep the cross-hairs of his sight on the target to ensure a hit. This missile itself weighs 59lbs (26.7kg) and has a single-stage solid-propellant motor which has a burn time of 1.18 seconds. Once the missile leaves the gun/missile-launcher, four fins at the rear of the missile unfold and it is guided to the target by a two-way infra-red command link which eliminates the need for the gunner to estimate the lead and range of the target. A Sheridan normally carries eight missiles and 20 rounds of ammunition, but this mix can be adjusted as required. In addition, 1,000 rounds of 0.5in and 3,000 rounds of 7.62mm ammunition are carried. The Sheridan is provided with a flotation screen, and when erected this enables the vehicle to propel itself across rivers and streams by its tracks. In 1978 it was announced that the M551 would be withdrawn from American service except in the 82nd Airborne Division, with headquarters at Fort Bragg, North Carolina.

Below: One of the prototypes of the Sheridan fires a Shillelagh missile during trials. The missile has an effective range of 2,500m against moving targets and 3,000m against static targets.

Merkava Mk 1 Main Battle Tank

Country of origin: Israel.
Armament: One 105mm gun; one 7.62mm machine-gun co-axial with main armament; one 7.62mm anti-aircraft fire control system.
Armour: Classified.
Dimensions: Length (gun forward) 27ft (8.25m); length (hull) 23ft 4in (7.12m); width 11ft 2in (3.4m); height (commander's cupola) 8ft 9in (2.66m).
Weight: (combat) 127,890lbs (58,000kg).
Engine: Teledyne Continental AVDS-1790-5A V-12 diesel developing 900hp.
Performance: Road speed 28mph (45kmh); range 249–311 miles (400–500km); vertical obstacle 2.99ft (0.914m); trench 10.5ft (3.2m); gradient 60 per cent.
History: Entered service with Israeli Army in 1978, to be succeeded in production by Merkava Mk 2.
(Note: the above specification is provisional)

Israel started to design an indigenous MBT in the late 1960s and, after many years of speculation, she announced in 1977 that she had indeed developed an MBT called the Merkava (Chariot) which would enter service the following year. The layout of the Merkava is unconventional with the engine and transmission at the front, the driver towards the front on the left and the fighting compartment at the rear. The engine is an American Teledyne Continental AVDS-1790-5A which is a more powerful version of that installed in the M60s used in some numbers by the Israeli Army, and this engine is coupled to an Allison CD-850-6B transmission. The suspension and road wheels are similar to those fitted to the Centurions used by the Israeli Army. There are six road wheels with the drive sprocket at the front, idler at the rear and return rollers, and the tops of the tracks are covered by steel covers to protect the suspension from damage from HEAT attack.

The turret has a very small cross section and a well sloped front and is difficult to hit when the tank is in a hull down position. The commander and gunner are seated on the right and the loader on the left, with both the commander and loader provided with a hatch in the roof.

Main armament consists of the well tried British 105mm L7 series rifled tank gun which is fitted with a fume extractor and a thermal sleeve. This gun

Above: Israel, with much armoured warfare experience, designed the Merkava to afford maximum protection over its frontal arc without reducing mobility to an unacceptable level.

is manufactured under licence in Israel and is also installed in the Israeli Centurion, M48 and M60 tanks. The gun has an elevation of +20° and a depression of −10°; when in a non-combat area the gun is held in position by a travelling lock. In addition to firing all of the standard 105mm projectiles the gun will fire a new APFSDS projectile developed by Israel Military Industries. The fire control system of the Merkava has been developed by Elbit Computers Limited and incorporates a ballistic computer, sensors and a laser rangefinder. One 7.62mm machine-gun is mounted co-axial with the main armament and another is mounted on the roof for anti-aircraft defence.

Standard equipment includes night vision devices, NBC system and a fire suppression system. The initial production version is the Mk1 which is being produced at the Israeli Ordnance facilities at Tel a Shumer, near Tel Aviv. This will be succeeded in production by the Mk2 which is expected to have a more powerful engine and a hydro-pneumatic suspension system. Much of the funding for the recent development of the Merkava has been provided by the United States.

Below: Merkava MBT from the rear clearly showing overall layout of this unconventional tank designed by General Tal.

Panzerjager K 4KH7FA SK 105 Light Tank/Tank Destroyer

Country of origin: Austria.
Crew: 3.
Armament: One 105mm gun; one 7.62mm machine gun co-axial with main armament; three smoke dischargers either side of turret.
Armour: 0.4–1.6in (10–40mm).
Dimensions: Length (with gun forwards) 25ft 6in (7.763m); length (hull) 18ft 3in (5.58m); width 8ft 2in (2.5m); height 8ft 2in (2.51m).
Weight: (combat) 38,587lbs (17,500kg).
Ground pressure: 0.68kg/cm².
Engine: Steyr 7FA turbo-charged 6-cylinder diesel developing 320hp at 2300rpm.
Performance: Road speed 40.4mph (65kmh); range 323 miles (520km); vertical obstacle 2ft 8in (0.8m); trench 7ft 11in (2.41m); gradient 75 per cent.
History: Entered service with Austrian Army in 1973/74. In service with Austria, Tunisia and other countries. Still in production.

In 1965 Saurer-Werke commenced the development of this well armed and highly mobile tank destroyer to meet the requirements of the Austrian Army. The chassis uses many components of an earlier range of APCs but its layout is quite different with the driver's compartment at the front, turret in the centre and the engine and transmission at the rear. The hull is all of welded construction and provides the crew with protection from small arms fire and shell splinters. The suspension is of the torsion bar type and consists of five dual rubber tyred road wheels with the drive sprocket at the rear, idler at the front and three track return rollers. The first and last road wheel stations have an hydraulic shock absorber.

The FL-12 turret is made under licence in Austria from the French company Fives-Lille-Cail and is identical to that fitted to the AMX-13 light tank and the Brazilian EE-17(6×6) tank destroyer. This turret is of the oscillating type with the 105mm gun fixed in the upper half which in turn pivots on the lower part. The gun can be elevated from −6° to +13° and the turret traversed through a full 360° in 12 to 15 seconds. The 105mm gun is fed from two revolver type magazines in the turret bustle, each of which holds six rounds of ammunition. Empty cartridge cases are ejected outside of the

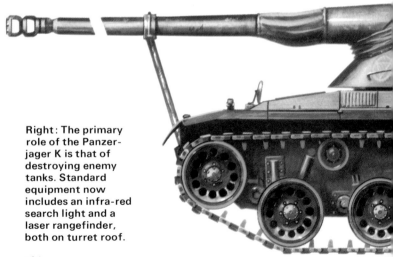

Right: The primary role of the Panzerjager K is that of destroying enemy tanks. Standard equipment now includes an infra-red search light and a laser rangefinder, both on turret roof.

turret through a small trap door in the turret rear. The two magazines have enabled the crew to be reduced to three men — commander, gunner and driver — and also allow a high rate of fire to be achieved for a short period; on the other hand once the 12 rounds have been fired at least one of the crew has to leave the vehicle to carry out manual reloading of the two magazines. A total of 44 rounds of 105mm ammunition are carried, which can be a mixture of the following types: HE with the complete round weighing 41lbs (18.4kg), HEAT with the complete round weighing 39lbs (17.7kg) which will penetrate 14in (360mm) of armour at an incidence of 0° or 6in (150mm) of armour at an incidence of 65°, smoke with the complete round weighing 42lbs (19.1kg). Mounted co-axial to the right of the main armament is a 7.62mm MG42/49 machine gun and mounted on either side of the turret are three electrically operated smoke dischargers; a total of 2000 rounds of 7.62mm ammunition are carried. Recently most vehicles have been fitted with an laser rangefinder mounted externally on the turret roof and above this has been mounted an infra-red/white-light searchlight. The Kürassier K, as the vehicle is often called, has no NBC system and no deep fording capability.

Above: Panzerjager K firing its 105mm gun. The empty cartridge cases are ejected out through a door in rear of the turret.

PT-76 Light Amphibious Tank

Country of origin: Soviet Union.
Crew: 3.
Armament: One 76.2mm gun; one 7.62mm machine gun co-axial with main armament.
Armour: 14mm (0.55in) maximum.
Dimensions: Length (gun forwards) 25ft (7.625m); length (hull) 22ft 8in (6.91m); width 10ft 4in (3.14m); height 7ft 2in (2.195m).
Weight: Combat 30,865lbs (14,000kg).
Ground pressure: 6.8lb/in² (0.48kg/cm²).
Power to weight ratio: 17.1hp/t.
Performance: Road speed 27.34mph (44km/h); water speed 6.2mph (10km/h); range 162 miles (260km); vertical obstacle 3ft 8in (1.1m); trench 9ft 2in (2.8m); gradient 60 per cent.
History: Entered service in 1952. In service with Afghanistan, Angola, China, Congo, Cuba, Czechoslovakia, East Germany, Egypt, Finland, Hungary, India, Indonesia, Iraq, Israel, Laos, North Korea, Pakistan, Poland, Soviet Union, Syria, Uganda, Vietnam and Yugoslavia. Production completed in early 1960s.

The Russians have been using amphibious tanks since the early 1920s. The PT-76 (*Plavaushiy Tank*) is based on the *Pinguin* cross-country vehicle. Since it entered service with the Russian Army in 1952, it has been exported to many countries and has seen combat in Africa, the Middle East and the Far East. It has a hull of all-welded steel construction. The driver is seated at the front of the hull, with the commander/gunner and loader in the turret, and the engine and transmission at the rear of the hull. The PT-76 is armed with a 76.2mm gun, this having an elevation of +30° and a depression of −4°. A 7.62mm SGMT machine-gun is mounted co-axially with the main armament. Forty rounds of 76.2mm and 1,000 rounds of 7.62mm ammunition are carried. The most outstanding feature of the PT-76 is its amphibious capability. It is propelled in the water by two water-jets, one in each side of the hull, with their exits in the hull rear. Before entering the water a trim vane is erected at the front of the hull and the driver's centre periscope is raised so that he can see over the top of the trim vane. The PT-76 has been built in large numbers and its basic chassis has been used for a whole family

Above right: PT-76 Model 2s show their amphibious capabilities: note trim vane erected, driver's periscope extended and schnorkel on the rear of the turret.

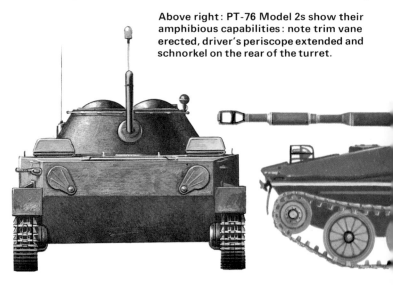

of armoured vehicles including the BTR-50 armoured personnel carrier, ASU-85 air-portable anti-tank gun, ZSU-23-4 self-propelled anti-aircraft gun, SA-6 'Gainful' anti-aircraft missile system, BMP-1 MICV, 'Frog' 2, 3, 4 and 5 tactical missile systems, GSP amphibious ferry, SP-74 122mm SPG and MT-LB vehicle to name just a few. A modified version has been built in ▶

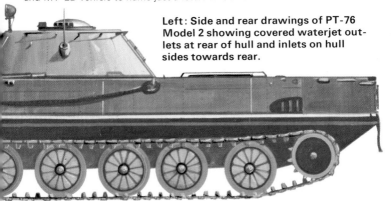

Left: Side and rear drawings of PT-76 Model 2 showing covered waterjet outlets at rear of hull and inlets on hull sides towards rear.

Above: PT-76 and motorcycle combination team being used in the reconnaissance role receive their orders by hand from 'Hoplite' helicopter (many Soviet AFVs are not fitted with radios).

China as the Type 63. This has a similar hull to the PT-76 but has a new turret mounting an 85mm gun and a co-axial 7.62mm machine-gun; there is also a 12.7mm anti-aircraft machine-gun on the roof. Although well over 20 years old, the PT-76 is still a useful vehicle in the reconnaissance role.

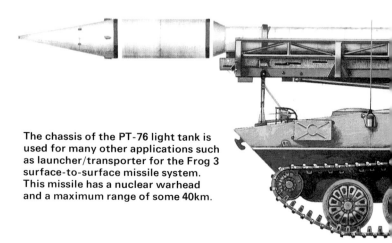

The chassis of the PT-76 light tank is used for many other applications such as launcher/transporter for the Frog 3 surface-to-surface missile system. This missile has a nuclear warhead and a maximum range of some 40km.

Above: In addition to being used by the Soviet Army the PT-76 is also used by the Soviet Marines and some 20 other countries.

Pz 68 Main Battle Tank

Pz 58, Pz 61, Pz 68 Mk1, Pz 68 Mk2, Pz 68 Mk3, Pz 68 Mk4, AA Tank, SPG and bridgelayer.
Country of origin: Switzerland.
Crew: 4.
Armament: One 105mm gun; one 7.5mm machine-gun co-axial with main armament; one 7.5mm anti-aircraft machine-gun; three smoke dischargers on each side of turret.
Armour: 60mm (2.36in) maximum.
Dimensions: Length (including main armament) 31ft 1½in (9.49m); length (hull only) 22ft 8in (6.9m); width 10ft 3½in (3.14m); height (overall) 9ft (2.75m).
Weight: Combat 87,523lbs (39,700kg).
Ground pressure: 12.23lb/in² (0.86kg/cm²).
Engine: MTU MB 837 eight-cylinder diesel developing 704hp at 2,200rpm.
Performance: Maximum road speed 34mph (55km/h); road range 186 miles (300km); vertical obstacle 2ft 6in (0.75m); trench 8ft 6in (2.6m); gradient 60 per cent.
History: Entered service with the Swiss Army in 1971 and still in service.

Shortly after the end of World War I, the Swiss purchased two Renault FT-17 light tanks for trials. These were followed in 1934 by four British Carden-Loyd tankettes. Just before World War II, Switzerland ordered some Czech CTH light tanks, to be assembled in Switzerland and fitted with Swiss armament and engines. By the time Czechoslovakia was overrun by the Germans only 24 tanks were in service with the Swiss Army under the designation Pz 39. In 1944 the Swiss built the prototype of a self-propelled anti-tank gun called the NKI, this being followed in 1945 by the NKII

assault gun. Neither of these vehicles entered production. Between 1947 and 1952 158 *Jagdpanzer* 38 (*t*) anti-tank guns were obtained from Czechoslovakia, and these remained in service until quite recently. Other post-war purchases included 200 AMX-13 light tanks and 300 Centurion MBTs, all of which are still in service today. In the early 1950s design work started on a Swiss main battle tank, and the first prototype, the Pz 58, was completed in 1958. Main armament consisted of a Swiss 90mm gun. The second prototype was completed the following year, and this was armed with a British 20-pounder gun. Between 1960 and 1961 a further 10 pre-production tanks were built, and these were armed with the British 105mm L7 tank gun. These tanks were known under the designation Pz 61, and 150 examples were built between 1964 and 1966 at the Federal Engineering Works at Thun. The main armament consisted of a 105mm gun built under ▶

Above: Entp Pz 65 armoured recovery vehicle changes the power pack of a second Entp Pz 65. The A frame mounted at the front of the hull lifts a maximum load of some 15,000kg, and the vehicle has two winches and a dozer blade.

Left: The Pz 61 is armed with a 105mm L7 gun designed in Britain and made under licence in Switzerland. Unlike most other tanks, the 7.62mm AA MG of the Pz 61 is used by the loader rather than by the tank commander.

Above: The bridgelayer member of the Pz 61/68 family is called the Brücken panzer 68 and has a bridge some 18.23m in length.

licence in Switzerland; a 20mm Oerlikon cannon was mounted to the left of the main armament and a 7.5mm machine-gun was fitted on the loader's hatch for anti-aircraft defence. In most Western tanks the latter machine-gun is on the commander's hatch, but the Swiss decided, quite rightly, that the role of the commander is to command, not to operate machine-guns! Some 52 rounds of 105mm, 240 rounds of 20mm and 3,000 rounds of 7.5mm ammunition are carried. Between 1971 and 1974 170 of an improved model, the Pz 68, were built. The Pz 68 has an improved fire-control system and the main armament is stabilised in both the horizontal and vertical planes. The tank also has a slightly more powerful engine and a modified gearbox. The hull of the Pz 68 is of cast construction, as is the turret. The driver is seated in the front of the hull and the other three crew members in the turret, the commander and gunner on the right and the loader on the left. The engine, which is imported from Germany, is at the rear of the hull, as is the Swiss transmission. The suspension consists of six road wheels, with the drive sprocket at the rear and the idler at the front. There are three return rollers. Each of the road wheels is independently located and sprung by layers of Belleville washers. The Germans had a similar system towards the end of World War II, but the Pz 61/Pz 68 is the first tank with this suspension to be built in quantity. The main armament is a 105mm gun with an elevation of +21° and a depression of −10°; a 7.5mm machine-gun is mounted co-axially with the main armament and there is a similar machine-gun on the loader's hatch for anti-aircraft defence. Some 52 rounds of 105mm and 5,200 rounds of 7.5mm ammunition are carried. The tank is provided with an NBC system and infra-red driving lights, but no infra-red

searchlight is provided to enable the tank to engage targets at night. The Pz 68 can ford streams to a maximum depth of 3ft 8in (1.1m). The Pz 68 Mk1 was followed in production by the Mk2, 50 of which were built in 1977. This model was followed by the Mk3 which has all the improvements of the Mk1 and Mk2 but also has a slightly larger turret. The final model of the series is expected to be the Mk4. It was expected that the Swiss would design a new tank for the 1980s but late in 1979 it was announced that this would be too expensive and that Switzerland would probably procure its next MBT from abroad, the two contenders being the West German Leopard 2 and the American M1 (XM1). Currently undergoing trials is the anti-aircraft version of the Pz 68; this is a modified MBT chassis fitted with the same turret as that installed on the German Gepard self-propelled anti-aircraft gun which is armed with two 35mm cannon. There are a number of variants of the Pz 61 and Pz 68 in service with the Swiss Army. The armoured recovery vehicle is known as the *Entpannungspanzer* 65 and weighs 38.38 tons (39,000kg). This is provided with a dozer blade at the front of the hull, an 'A' frame which can lift a maximum of 14.76 tons (15,000kg) and two winches. The main winch has a capacity of 24.6 tons (25,000kg) and the secondary winch has a capacity of 0.49 tons (500kg). This model has a crew of five and is armed with a single 7.5mm machine-gun and smoke dischargers. The bridgelayer is known as the *Brückenpanzer* 68: this is provided with a one-piece aluminium bridge 59ft 10in (18.23m) in length taking about two minutes to lay and five minutes to retract. A prototype of a self-propelled gun called the *Panzer-Kanone* 68 was built in the early 1970s. This is essentially a Pz 68 chassis fitted with a new turret mounting a 155mm Swiss gun, which has a range of 18.6 miles (30km). A 7.5mm machine-gun is mounted on the roof for anti-aircraft defence and smoke dischargers are also provided.

Soltam L-33 155mm Self-propelled Gun/Howitzer

Country of origin: Israel.
Crew: 8.
Arment: One 155mm gun/howitzer; one 7.62mm anti-aircraft machine-gun.
Armour: 0.4–2.5in (12–64mm).
Dimensions: Length (with armament) 27ft 9in (8.47m); length (hull) 21ft 3in (6.47m); width 11ft 4in (3.45m); height 11ft 4in (3.45m).
Weight: (combat) 91,507lbs (41,500kg).
Engine: Cummins VT 8-460-B1 diesel developing 460hp at 2600rpm.
Performance: Road speed 22mph (36kmh); road range 161 miles (260km); vertical obstacle 2ft 11in (0.91m); trench 7ft 6in (2.3m); gradient 60 per cent.
History: Entered service with Israeli Army in 1970/71. Production complete.

In the late 1960s the Israeli Soltam Company started to develop a new self-propelled gun/howitzer for the Israeli Army. This had to be based on the Sherman chassis, provide all round protection for the crew, have a high rate of fire, have a good range and carry an adequate supply of onboard ammuni-

tion which could be easily replenished. After trials with prototype weapons the Soltam design was accepted for service with the Israeli Army as the L-33 (33 being the length of the ordnance in calibres).

The L-33 is essentially a much modified M4A3E8 Sherman tank chassis with the turret removed, engine moved forwards and a new all welded superstructure added. The driver is seated at the front of the hull on the left and the commander seated above and to his rear, both provided with bullet proof windows. An entry door is provided in each side of the hull and there are two hatches in the roof, one for the commander on the left and one for the anti-aircraft gunner on the right. Mounted at the anti-aircraft gunner's station is a 7.62mm machine gun with a traverse of 360°.

The 155mm gun/howitzer is mounted in the front of the vehicle and has a maximum elevation of +52°, a depression of −3° and a traverse of 30° left and 30° right, elevation and traverse both being manual. The ordnance, which is based on the M-68 towed gun/howitzer, has a fume extractor, single baffle muzzle brake and a pneumatic rammer which enables the weapon to be loaded at all angles of elevation. It fires an HE projectile weighing 96.35lbs (43.7kg) with a maximum muzzle velocity of 740 yards a second (725 metres a second) to a maximum range of 21,880 yards (20,000m); other types of ammunition that can be fired include smoke, practice and illuminating. A well trained crew can fire four rounds a minute for a short period and a total of 60 155mm projectiles are carried, of which 16 are for ready use. Doors are provided in the rear of the hull for the rapid resupply of ammunition.

Above: Soltam L-33 155mm Self-Propelled Gun/Howitzer from the rear with the ammunition resupply doors in the hull rear in open position. A total of 60 155mm projectiles and charges are carried of which 16 are ready for use. The weapon fires an HE projectile to a maximum range of 21,000 metres.

Left: Soltam L-33 155mm Self-Propelled Gun/Howitzer showing the weapon which is mounted in the forward part of the hull with an elevation of +52°, depression of −3°, and traverse of 30° left and right. The L-33 was first used by Israel during the 1973 Middle East War and is based on a Sherman hull.

Stridsvagn (S) 103
Main Battle Tank

Country of origin: Sweden.
Crew: 3.
Armament: One 105mm gun; one 7.62mm machine-gun on commander's cupola; two 7.62mm machine-guns on hull top; eight smoke dischargers.
Armour: Classified.
Dimensions: Length (including armament) 29ft 2in (8.9m); length (hull) 23ft (7m); width 11ft 2in (3.4m); height (overall) 8ft 2½in (2.5m).
Weight: Combat 85,980lbs (39,000kg).
Ground pressure: 12.8lb/in² (0.9kg/cm²).

Right, below and bottom: Side, rear and front views of the Bofors S tank which was designed in the late 1950s by Sven Berge of the Swedish Army Ordnance Department. 300 S tanks were built.

Engines: Rolls-Royce K.60 multi-fuel engine developing 240bhp at 3,650rpm; Boeing 553 gas turbine developing 490shp at 38,000rpm.
Performance: Maximum road speed 31mph (50km/h), water speed 4mph (6km/h); range 242 miles (390km); vertical obstacle 2ft 11in (0.9m); trench 7ft 7in (2.3m); gradient 60 per cent.
History: Entered service with the Swedish Army in 1966 and still in service.

Of all the tanks in service today, the 'S' tank is perhaps the most unusual and controversial. Its design dates back to the 1950s and is based on an original idea by Sven Berge of the Swedish Army Ordnance department. The main battle tank of the Swedish Army in the 1960s was to have been a tank called the KPV, armed with a 150mm smooth-bore gun. Two prototypes of this tank were completed by Landsverk, but these were never fitted with their turrets and armament. These, and a number of other tanks including a Sherman and an Ikv-103 assault gun, were then used to test the basic S ▶

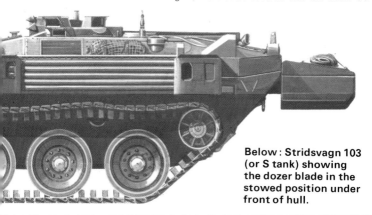

Below: Stridsvagn 103 (or S tank) showing the dozer blade in the stowed position under front of hull.

Above: Head-on view of S tank showing fixed 105mm gun which is a longer version of the British L7 gun.

Right: Well camouflaged S tank moves forwards during an exercise. On the commander's cupola is a 7.62mm MG.

tank concept. In 1958 Bofors was awarded a full development contract and the first two prototype S tanks were completed in 1961. These were powered by a gas turbine engine and an eight-cylinder petrol engine. Apart from the 105mm gun, they had five 7.62mm machine-guns; one on the commander's cupola and two in a box on each side of the hull firing forwards. Their suspension was also different from later models. These were followed by a pre-production batch of 10 tanks. First production tanks were completed in 1966, and 300 were eventually built, the last of them being completed in 1971. The other MBT of the Swedish Army is the British Centurion, of which 350 are in service. These are to be rebuilt in the near future. The S tank (or to give it the correct name, the *Stridsvagn* 103), has a crew of three (commander, driver/gunner and radio operator). The driver is seated on the left, with the radio operator behind him, facing the rear. The commander is on the right of the hull. The radio operator can drive the tank backwards if required, and the commander also has an accelerator and brake pedal. The tank is armed with a 105mm rifled tank gun which is fixed to the hull rather than mounted in a turret as in conventional tanks. This has not only enabled the overall height of the tank to be reduced, but has also allowed an automatic loader to be installed. The 105mm gun is a longer version of the famous British L7 series gun and is made in Sweden. The gun is fed from a magazine which holds 50 rounds of ammunition of the following types: Armour-Piercing Discarding Sabot, High-Explosive Squash-Head, Smoke and High Explosive. The empty cartridge cases are automatically ejected through a hatch in the rear of the hull. The tank can fire between 10 and 15 aimed rounds per minute. Some of the prototypes were fitted with a .5in ranging machine-gun, but production models have an optical range finder, and a laser rangefinder has now been developed. Two 7.62mm machine-guns are mounted in a box on the left of the hull, firing forwards, and there is a single 7.62mm machine-gun on the commander's cupola. The latter can be aimed and fired from within the vehicle. Some 2,750 rounds of 7.62mm machine-gun ammunition are carried. Eight smoke dischargers are provided,

Above: S tanks move forward with infantry support. Mounted around the top of the hull is a collapsible flotation screen which can be erected in 20 minutes and gives the tank an amphibious capability.

and some S tanks have been fitted with Bofors Lyran flare launchers so that they can engage targets at night. The suspension is of the hydro-pneumatic type, and consists of four road wheels (these are the same as those fitted to the Centurion tank), with the drive sprocket at the front and the idler at the rear, there being two track-return rollers. The gun is laid in elevation by the driver, who can adjust the suspension so that the gun can be elevated to +12° and depressed to −10°. It is aimed in traverse by slewing the tank in its tracks. When the gun is fired, the suspension is locked so as to provide a more stable firing platform. Another unusual feature of the tank is its power-pack, which is mounted in the forward part of the hull. This consists of two engines, a diesel and gas turbine. The diesel is the Rolls-Royce K.60, which is also used in the British FV432 APC and FV433 Abbot self-propelled gun, whilst the gas turbine is of American design but built in Belgium by FN. For normal operations the diesel is used, but in combat, or crossing very rough country, the gas turbine is also used. The first production models of the S tank (these were designated Strv. 103As) were not fitted with flotation screens, but these are standard on the Strv.103Bs, and all earlier tanks have now been refitted with them. The screen is carried collapsed around the top of the hull and takes about 15 minutes to erect. The tank is propelled in the water by its tracks. There are many lakes and rivers in Sweden too deep for schnorkel crossing, so the only practical solution was the fitting of the flotation screen. The tank is provided with infra-red driving lights but does not have an infra-red searchlight. A dozer blade is mounted at the front of the hull for the preparation of fire positions. The S tank has a very low silhouette compared with other main battle tanks, and its glacis plate is well sloped, giving the maximum amount of protection available. The S tank has been tested by a number of other countries including Great Britain and the United States, but no other country has placed a similar design in production. There are no variants of the S tank although components of the tank are used in the VK 155 self-propelled gun built by Bofors a few years ago, as well as the Bofors 40mm self-propelled anti-aircraft gun, development of which was stopped some years ago. Bofors and Hägglund and Söner have established a joint company to design a new Main Battle Tank which should enter service in the late 1980s. Bofors will be responsible for the armament and fire control system while Hägglund and Söner will be responsible for the chassis. It is expected that the tank will have a crew of three, weigh 35,000kg and have a maximum road speed of 70km/h. Armament will be a 105mm or a 120mm gun which will be provided with an automatic loader to enable a high rate of fire to be achieved and to keep to a three man crew as in the current Stridsvagn 103(S) Main Battle Tank.

T-10 Heavy Tank

T-10, T-10M
Country of origin: Soviet Union.
Crew: 4.
Armament: One 122mm gun; one 14.5mm machine-gun co-axial with main armament; one 14.5mm anti-aircraft machine-gun.
Armour: 20mm—250mm (0.79—10.8in).
Dimensions: Length (gun forward) 34ft 9in (10.6m); length (hull) 23ft 1in (7.04m); width 11ft 8in (3.566m); height 8ft (2.43m) without anti-aircraft machine-gun.
Weight: Combat 114,640lbs (52,000kg).
Ground pressure: 11.09lb/in² (0.78kg/cm²).
Engine: V-2-IS(V2K), 12-cylinder water-cooled diesel developing 700hp at 2,000rpm.
Performance: Road speed 26mph (42km/h); range 155 miles (250km); vertical obstacle 2ft 11in (0.9m); trench 9ft 10in (3m); gradient 60 per cent.
History: Entered service in 1957. In service with East Germany, Egypt, Soviet Union, Syria and Vietnam. Production completed in early 1960s. (Note: data above relate to T-10M.)

The standard Russian heavy tanks during the closing years of World War II were the IS series. The IS-4 entered service in small numbers in 1946—7 and further development resulted in the IS-5, IS-6, IS-7, IS-8, IS-9 and finally

Below: T-10M heavy tank from the rear; this particular tank does not have a sheet metal stowage box on the rear of the turret, but does have extra fuel tanks.

the IS-10. The last was placed in production in 1956 as the T-10. The tank has the same engine as the IS-3, but a more powerful gun and much improved armour layout. Today T-10s do not form a part of the normal equipment of Russian tank regiments or divisions, but are instead formed into special battalions and attached to divisions as required. The T-10 has a crew of four (commander, gunner, loader and driver). The driver is seated at the front of the vehicle with the other three crew members in the turret, the commander being on the left. The engine and transmission are at the rear of the hull. The suspension consists of seven road wheels (the IS series have six) with the idler at the front and the drive sprocket at the rear; there are three track-return rollers on each side. The first model to enter service was the T-10. This is armed with a 122mm gun and 12.7mm DShK anti-aircraft and co-axial machine-guns. The 122mm gun has an elevation of +17° and a depression of −3°, and a total of 30 rounds of 122mm ammunition of the separate loading type is carried, as well as 1,000 rounds of 12.7mm machine-gun ammunition. The T-10 fires two types of ammunition, an HE projectile which weighs 60lbs (27.3kg) and an APHE projectile which weighs 55lbs (25kg); both have a muzzle velocity of 2,904ft/s (885m/s). The APHE round will penetrate 7.3in (185mm) of armour at a range of 1,092 yards (1,000m). The 122mm gun has a maximum range of 18,154 yards (16,600m) with the gun at its maximum elevation, and its effective range in the anti-tank role is between 1,312 and 2,187 yards (1,200–2,000m). The T-10M is a further development of the T-10 and this has a number of major improvements to increase its combat effectiveness. The 12.7mm machine-guns have been replaced by 14.5mm KPVT (co-axial) and KPV (anti-aircraft) machine guns. The double baffle muzzle-brake on the T-10 has been replaced by a multi-baffle muzzle-brake, but the fume extractor has been retained. The main armament is now stabilised in both planes, eg elevation and traverse. In addition to the HE and APHE rounds the 122mm gun can fire a HEAT round with a muzzle velocity of 2,953ft/s (900m/s), which will penetrate 18in (460mm) of armour. The basic T-10 is provided with infra-red driving lights, but in addition the T-10M has an infra-red searchlight on the commander's cupola; there is another infra-red searchlight mounted to the right of the main armament, and this moves in elevation with the main armament. The T-10 can ford to a depth of 3ft 11in (1.2m) without preparation, but the T-10M can be provided with a schnorkel for deep fording operations. The T-10M is also provided with an NBC system and many have been fitted with a large stowage box of sheet metal welded to the turret rear. Additional fuel tanks can be fitted at the rear of the hull to increase the operating range of the tank. The T-10 has been used by Egypt

Above: The T-10 was developed in the early 1950s and made its first public appearance at the November 1957 Moscow parade.

and Syria in the 1973 Middle East campaign. It is normally used to provide long-range anti-tank support to the T-55/T-62 tanks. It would also be used to spearhead a breakthrough on a vital sector, where its firepower and armour would prove most useful. The T-10 does have a number of drawbacks. First, it is slightly slower than the T-62 and T-55 MBTs, which could mean that an advance has to slow down to allow the T-10s to keep place. Second, as with most Russian tanks, the T-10's gun has a very limited depression, making it difficult to fire from reverse slopes. And third, its ammunition is of the separate loading type (eg projectile and separate cartridge case), which takes a little longer to load and therefore reduces the tank's rate of fire to three or four rounds per minute. The T-10 has excellent armour, and is the most difficult of all current Russian tanks to destroy.

T-54/T-55 Main Battle Tank

T-54/T-55, ARV, bridgelayer and mine-clearance tank
Country of origin: Soviet Union.
Crew: 4.
Armament: One 100mm gun; one 7.62mm SGMT machine-gun co-axial with main armament; one 7.62mm SGMT machine-gun in bow of tank; one 12.7mm DShK anti-aircraft machine-gun.
Armour: 170mm (6.7in) maximum.
Dimensions: Length (including armament) 29ft 6in (9m); length (hull) 21ft 2in (6.45m); width 10ft 9in (3.27m); height (without anti-aircraft armament) 7ft 10in (2.4m).
Weight: Combat 79.366lbs (36,000kg).
Ground pressure: 11.52lb/in^2 (0.81kg/cm^2).
Engine: Model V-54 12-cylinder air-cooled diesel developing 520hp at 2,000rpm.
Performance: Maximum road speed 30mph (48km/h); range 249 miles (400km); vertical obstacle 2ft 8in (0.8m); trench 8ft 10in (2.7m); gradient 60 per cent.
History: Entered service with the Russian Army in 1950. Also used by Afghanistan, Albania, Algeria, Angola, Bangladesh, Bulgaria, Communist China, Cuba, Cyprus, Czechoslovakia, East Germany, Egypt, Ethiopia,

Below: The T-55 entered service in late 1950s and was first seen in public in 1961. Major improvements include a more power-ful engine, armament stabilised in both planes and more ammunition carried.

Finland, Guinea, Hungary, India, Iraq, Israel, Libya, Mongolia, Morocco, Mozambique, North Korea, North Yemen, Pakistan, Peru, Poland, Romania, Somalia, South Yemen, Sudan, Syria, Uganda, Vietnam, Yugoslavia and Zambia. (Note data refer to T-54.)

The first prototype of the T-54 was completed in 1947. This was a logical development of the T-44 tank developed towards the end of World War II. The latter tank was in turn a development of the T-34 which is considered by many to be the best medium tank of the war. The T-54 has also been built in China as the T-59 as well as in Czechoslovakia and Poland. No accurate production figures of the T-54/T-55 have been released but it is likely that between 60,000 and 70,000 of all models of the T-54 and T-55 have been built. The hull of the T-54 is of all-welded construction and the turret is cast, with the top then welded into position. The driver is seated at the front of the hull on the right, with the other three crew members in the turret. The commander and gunner are on the left with the loader on the right. Two hatches are provided. The engine and transmission are at the rear of the hull, separated from the fighting compartment by a bulkhead. The suspension consists of five road wheels per side, with the drive sprocket at the front and the idler at the rear. There are no return rollers as the top of the track rests on the tops of the road wheels. The suspension is of the well-tried torsion-bar type. Main armament consists of a 100mm D-10T rifled tank gun firing APHE, HEAT or HE rounds. The gun is capable of an elevation of +17° and a depression of −4°. The latter is one of the major drawbacks of the tank compared with Western tanks. A 7.62mm SGMT machine-gun is mounted co-axially with the main armament, and there is a similar weapon in the front of the hull, operated by the driver. A 12.7mm DShK machine-gun is mounted on the loader's hatch for use in the anti-aircraft role. Some 34 rounds of 100mm, 500 rounds of 12.7mm and 3,000 rounds of 7.62mm ammunition are carried. Most T-54 and T-55 tanks have a full range of night-vision equipment of the infra-red type, including driving lights, commander's searchlight and search-light to the right of the main armament. Additional fuel tanks can be fitted to the rear of the hull to increase the operating range of the tank. The tank ▶

Right: Front and rear views of T-54 tank as used by Egyptian Army during the 1967 Middle East War. The 12.7mm DShK AA MG is mounted on the loader's cupola and can be traversed 360°.

Right: A well worn T-55 tank. Like most Soviet tanks, all T-54/T-55s can lay a smoke screen by injecting diesel fuel into their exhaust pipes on either side of the hull of the tank.

Below right: The Soviet Union provided China with a number of T-54 tanks in the early 1950s and China subsequently built this tank under the designation of the T-59 (or Type 59).

can also lay its own smoke-screen in a similar fashion to the PT-76 by injecting vaporised diesel fuel into the exhaust system on either side of the tank. The tank can ford to a maximum depth of 4ft 7in (1.4m) without preparation, and with the aid of a schnorkel it can ford to a depth of 18ft (5.486m). Most tanks can be fitted with a dozer blade on the front of the hull. When first introduced, the T-54 did not have an NBC system. Late production models have one installed, however, as do T-55s. There are at least five models of the T-54 differing in minor detail; the T-54 (early), T-54, T-54A, T-54B and T-54C. In 1960 there appeared the T-55, with many improvements over the T-54 including a more powerful 580hp engine, increased armament, no anti-aircraft machine-gun (this was subsequently fitted to most T-55s). The T-55A followed in 1963; this had no bow machine-gun and the co-axial 7.62mm SGMT was replaced by a PKT machine-gun. The basic T-54/T-55 has been adopted for a wide range of roles. There are at least four different armoured recovery vehicles, these being known as the T-54-T, T-54A ARV, T-54B ARV and the T-54C ARV. The most common model is the T-54-T which has a spade at the rear, a platform for carrying spare tank components and a jib crane. A schnorkel can be mounted for deep fording operations. Two basic types of mine-clearing tank are in service, one being of the plough type and the other of the roller type. (There are a number of different types of the latter.) Three bridgelayers are in service. The first of these to enter service was the MTU-54/MTU-55, which carries a bridge 40ft 4in (12.3m) in length. The MTU-20 has a bridge whose ends fold up when the vehicle is moving. When opened out this bridge can span a gap of up to 65ft 7in (20m). The Czechs have developed a model called the MT-55, which has a scissors type bridge which can be used to span gaps of up to 55ft 9in (17m). East Germany has developed the BLG-60 bridgelayer, which is of the scissors type and when opened out can span a gap of up to 22 yards (20m). The latest variant to appear on the T-54/T-55 chassis is the IMR Combat Engineer Vehicle, which has a dozer blade mounted at the front of the hull and a hydraulically operated crane that can be traversed through a full 360 degrees. Components of the T-54 are also used in the ZSU-57-2 twin 57mm anti-aircraft tank, the ATS-59 tracked tractor and the PTS amphibian. Further development of the tank has resulted in the T-62 main battle tank. The T-54 has been used in combat by North Vietnam, Pakistan, India, Egypt, Syria, Iraq, Angola, Algeria, Libya and Somalia, and has proved to be a reliable tank in service.

T-62 Main Battle Tank

T-62, T-62A
Country of origin: Soviet Union.
Crew: 4.
Armament: One 115mm U-5TS gun; one 7.62mm PKT machine-gun co-axial with main armament; one 12.7mm DShK anti-aircraft machine-gun (optical).
Armour: 20mm–170mm (0.79–6.80in).
Dimensions: Length (overall) 30ft 7in (9.33m); length (hull) 21ft 9in (6.63m); width 11ft (3.35m); height (without anti-aircraft machine-gun) 7ft 10in (2.4m).
Weight: Combat 88,200lbs (40,000kg).
Ground pressure: 10.24lb/in^2 (0.72kg/cm^2).
Engine: Model V-2-62 12-cylinder water-cooled diesel engine developing 580hp at 2,000rpm.
Performance: Road speed 28mph (45.5kmh); range (without additional fuel tanks) 280 miles (450km); vertical obstacle 2ft 8in (0.8m); trench 9ft 2in (2.8m); gradient 60 per cent.
History: Entered service with the Russian Army in 1963. In service with Afghanistan, Algeria, Bulgaria, Cuba, Egypt, India, Iraq, Israel, Libya, North Korea, Soviet Union and Syria. Still being built.

Above: The T-62 can ford to a depth of 1.4m without preparation, and to a depth of 5.5m with a snorkel fitted. Clearly shown in this photograph is the small door in the rear of the turret, through which the spent 115mm cartridge cases are ejected, and the long range fuel tanks at hull rear.

Right: Standard equipment on the T-62 includes an NBC system and night vision equipment including infra-red driving light, infra-red searchlight to the right of the main armament and infra-red search-light on the commander's cupola that can be operated from within the turret.

Above: A column of T-62s trundles past a motor-cycle reconnaissance team on exercise in the Soviet Union.

The T-62 was developed in the late 1950s as the successor to the earlier T-54/T-55 series, and was first seen in public in May 1965. In appearance it is very similar to the earlier T-54. It does, however, have a longer and wider hull, a new turret and main armament, and can easily be distinguished from the T-54 as the latter has a distinct gap between its first and second road wheels, whereas the T-62's road wheels are more evenly spaced, and the T-62's gun is provided with a bore evacuator. The hull of the T-62 is of all-welded construction with the glacis plate being 4in (100mm) thick. The turret is of cast armour, and this varies in thickness from 6.7in (170mm) at ▶

Fully closed down
T-62 tanks on the advance.
The 115mm smooth bore gun
can fire APFSDS, HEAT and
HE rounds at a maximum of
four rounds per minute ; some
40 rounds of 115mm
ammunition are carried.

129

the front to 2.4in (60mm) at the rear. The driver is seated at the front of the hull on the left side, with the other three crew members in the turret, the commander and gunner on the left and the loader on the right. The engine and transmission are at the rear of the hull. The suspension is of the well tried torsion-bar type, and consists of five road wheels with the idler at the front and the drive sprocket at the rear. The U-5TS gun is of the smooth-bore type, and has an elevation of +17° and a depression of −4°. A 7.62mm PKT machine-gun is mounted co-axially with the main armament. When the T-62 first entered service it did not have an anti-aircraft machine-gun, but in the last few years many T-62s have been provided with the standard 12.7mm DShK weapon which is mounted on the loader's cupola, T-62s thus fitted being designated T-62A. Three types of ammunition are carried − High Explosive, Fin-Stabilised Armour-Piercing Discarding Sabot (FSAPDS) and High Explosive Anti-Tank (HEAT). The FSAPDS round has a muzzle velocity of 5,512ft/s (1,680m/s) and an effective range of 1,749 yards (1,600m). When this round is fired the sabot (the disposable 'slipper' around the projectile) drops off after the round has left the barrel and the fins of the projectile unfold to stabilise the round in flight. According to Israeli reports, this round will penetrate 11.8in (300mm) of armour at a range of 1,094 yards (1,000m). The 115mm round is manually loaded but once the gun has been fired the gun automatically returns to a set angle at

Below: T-62 tank crews "scramble" on exercise. In a real emergency, such a formation would be extremely vulnerable.

which the empty cartridge case is ejected from the breech, after which it moves onto a chute and is then thrown out through a small hatch in the turret rear. It would appear that this is a somewhat unreliable system. The tank has an average rate of fire of four rounds per minute, and a stabiliser is provided to stabilise the gun in both elevation and traverse. A total of 40 rounds of 115mm and 2,500 rounds of 7.62mm ammunition is carried. The T-62 is provided with an NBC system, infra-red driving lights, infra-red searchlight on the commander's cupola and an infra-red searchlight to the right of the main armament, moving in elevation with the main armament, to allow the T-62 to enlarge targets at night. The tank can ford streams to a depth of 4ft 7in (1.4m) without preparation. A 'schnorkel' can be erected on the loader's hatch, held in the upright position by stays. When fitted with this device the tank can ford to a maximum depth of 18 feet (5.486m). When not required the schnorkel is carried on the rear of the tank in sections. Like the T-55, the T-62 can lay its own smoke screen, this being achieved by injecting vaporised diesel fuel into the exhaust pipes on each side of the hull. Additional fuel tanks can be mounted at the rear of the hull in order to increase the operating range of the tank, these being jettisoned by the driver before the tank goes into action. The T-62 has been used in combat by the Egyptian and Syrian forces. Although not so sophisticated as western tanks, the T-62 has proved itself a rugged and reliable vehicle. It is estimated that at least 40,000 T-62 tanks have been built in the Soviet Union, although unlike the earlier T-54/T-55, production of the tank has not been undertaken in either Czechoslovakia or Poland.

T-64 and T-72 Main Battle Tanks

Country of origin: Soviet Union.
Crew: 3.
Armament: One 125mm gun; one 7.62mm PKT machine-gun co-axial with main armament; one 12.7mm anti-aircraft machine-gun.
Armour: Not available.
Dimensions: Length (including armament) 29ft 7in (9.02m); length (hull) 21ft (6.4m); width 11ft 1in (3.375m); height (commander's cupola) 7ft 5in (2.265m).
Weight: Combat 90,405lbs (41,000kg).
Engine: 780hp diesel.
Performance: Road speed 50mph (80kmh); range 310 miles (500km); vertical obstacle 3ft (0.915m); trench 8ft 10in (2.7m); gradient 60 per cent.
History: Entered service with Soviet Army in 1972 and also in service with East Germany and Syria.

In the 1960s the Soviets built prototypes of the M1970 MBT. The unusual suspension consisted of six small road wheels with the idler at the front, drive sprocket at the rear and three or four track return rollers. The M1970 had a turret similar to that of the T-62 and is thought to have been armed with the same 115mm smooth bore gun as the T-62. The M1970 was not placed in production, but a further development, called the T-64, was and this entered service with the Soviet Army in the late 1960s. The T-64 has a similar hull and suspension to the M1970 but has a new turret armed with a 125mm smooth bore gun which is fed from an automatic loader — this has made the loader redundant so reducing the crew from four to three men, commander, gunner and driver.

In 1972 another new tank entered production in the Soviet Union. This is called the T-72 and has the same armament with an automatic loader as the earlier T-64, but a slightly different hull and turret. The major difference between the T-64 and the T-72 is their suspension: the latter's consists of six large road wheels with the drive sprocket at the rear, idler at the front

Below: The T-64 preceded the T-72 in production but is used only by the Soviet Army. It has the same 125mm gun with an automatic loader as the T-72 but has different suspension and a slightly different turret.

132

and three return rollers. Over the forward part of the track on either side are four removable spring loaded skirt plates which, when in action are un-clipped and spring forward at an angle of some 60 degrees from the side of the vehicle to give some protection from ATGWs.

The 125mm smooth bore gun fires fin-stabilised APDS, HE and HEAT projectiles and some 40 rounds are carried. The APDS projectile is believed to have a muzzle velocity of some 1,860 yards a second (1,700 metres a second) and an effective range of 2,188–3,282 yards (2,000–3,000m). A 7.62mm PKT machine-gun is mounted co-axial with the main armament and a new 12.7mm machine-gun is mounted at the commander's station for use in the anti-aircraft role. The fire control system is believed to include a laser rangefinder. Standard equipment includes an NBC system, a full range of night vision equipment, snorkel for deep wading and a dozer blade which is mounted under the hull. Main improvements over the T-62 are in the areas of firepower and mobility, although some sources have stated that the T-72 has improved armour with similar capability to that of the British invented Chobham armour. The T-72 is now being produced at the rate of over 2,000 a year and is expected to be produced in Poland and Czechoslovakia, so becoming the standard MBT of the Warsaw Pact.

Above: The T-72 entered produc-tion in 1972 and is already in service with East Germany, Syria and the Soviet Union. Production is expected to commence in Czechoslovakia and Poland in the near future.

TAM Medium Tank

Country of origin: Argentina.
Crew: 4.
Armament: One 105mm gun; one 7.62mm machine gun co-axial with main armament; one 7.62mm anti-aircraft machine gun; eight smoke dischargers.
Armour: Classified.
Dimensions: Length (with gun forwards) 27ft (8.23m); length (hull) 22ft 3in (6.775m); width 10ft 8in (3.25m); height (without AA MG) 7ft 11in (2.42m).
Weight: (combat) 67,252lbs (30,500kg).
Ground pressure: 0.79kg/cm².
Engine: MTU supercharged 6-cylinder diesel developing 710hp at 2200rpm.
Performance: Road speed 46mph (75kmh); road range 342 miles (550km); vertical obstacle 3ft 3in (1m); trench 8ft 2in (2.5m); gradient 60 per cent.
History: Entering production for Argentinian Army.

The Argentinian Army has in the past obtained most of its equipment from the United States but recent American policy has led to a drastic curtailment in the supply of arms to many countries, especially those in South America. So in 1974 the Argentinian Army placed a contract with the West German company of Thyssen Henschel for the design and development of the TAM (Tanque Argentino Mediano) medium tank, and a contract was placed at the same time for the design and development of an infantry fighting vehicle to operate with the TAM, called the VCI (Véhiculo Combate Infanteria). Under the terms of the contract three prototypes of both the TAM and the VCI were to be supplied and a factory was to be established in Argentina to undertake production of both vehicles, which would initially be assembled from components supplied from West Germany but in time would be mostly manufactured in Argentina, not only providing some employment but also saving valuable foreign exchange costs.

Both the TAM and the VCI are based to a large extent on the chassis of the Marder Mechanised Infantry Combat Vehicle which entered service with the West German Army in 1971. The hull of the TAM is all of welded steel construction with the driver seated at the front of the well-sloped hull on

Above: The TAM Medium Tank has an operational range of 550km which can be increased to 900km by fitting two auxiliary fuel tanks at the rear.

Right: TAM Medium Tank is essentially a Marder Mechanised Infantry Combat Vehicle hull with a new turret and a 105mm gun mounted at the rear of the hull.

Above: The TAM Medium Tank was developed by Thyssen Henschel of West Germany to meet the requirements of the Argentinian Army.

the left with the engine to his right. The all welded turret is mounted at the rear of the hull with the commander and gunner on the right and the loader on the left. The suspension system is of the torsion bar type and consists of six dual rubber tyred road wheels with the drive sprocket at the front, idler at the rear and three track return rollers. The first, second, fifth and sixth road wheel stations are provided with a hydraulic shock absorber. The basic model has a range on internal fuel tanks of some 342 miles (550km) but to increase the range to 559 miles (900km) two long range fuel tanks can be mounted at the rear of the hull. The basic vehicle can ford to a depth of 4ft 7in (1.4m) without any preparation but with a snorkel fitted it can ford to a depth of 13ft 2in (4m).

Main armament consists of a 105mm gun which can fire fixed APFSDS, HEAT, HE-T, HESH and WP-T rounds, with a total of 50 rounds being carried, and loaded into the TAM via a door in the rear of the hull or via a small circular door in the left side of the turret. A 7.62mm machine gun is mounted co-axial with the main armament and a similar weapon is mounted on the turret roof for anti-aircraft defence; four electrically operated smoke dischargers are fitted either side of the turret. The fire control system consists of a panoramic sight for the commander which has a magnification of from x6 to x20, a coincidence rangefinder which is also operated by the commander while the gunner has a sight with a magnification of x8.

Type 60 Self-propelled Recoilless Rifle

Country of origin: Japan.
Crew: 3.
Armament: Two 106mm recoilless rifles, one .5in ranging machine-gun.
Armour: 15mm (0.59in) maximum.
Dimensions: Length 14ft 1in (4.3m); width 7ft 7in (2.23m); height 4ft 6in (1.38m).
Weight: Combat 17,640lbs (8,000kg).
Ground pressure: $0.67kg/cm^2$.
Engine: Komatsu T120 six-cylinder air-cooled diesel developing 120hp at 2,400rpm.
Performance: Maximum road speed 28mph (45kmh); range 80 miles (130km); vertical obstacle 1ft 10in (0.55m); trench 5ft 10in (1.78m); gradient 60 per cent.
History: Entered service with the Japanese SDF (Army) in 1960.

The Type 60 self-propelled recoilless rifle fulfils a role similar to that of the American M50 ONTOS (no longer in service) and the French Light Fighting Unit (tested by the French Army but not adopted). All three vehicles were developed in the 1950s. They are all lightly armoured and are designed to destroy enemy tanks with their recoilless rifles. For survival each vehicle

relies on its small size and manoeuvrability. Design work on the Type 60 started in 1954 and prototypes were built by Komatsu (SS1) and Mitsubishi (SS2). These were tested in 1955 and had the distinction of being the first Japanese armoured fighting vehicles to be completed after the end of World War II. These were not considered satisfactory, so further prototypes were constructed, these being known as the SS3 and SS4. The latter was standardised as the Type 60 Self-Propelled Recoilless Rifle and production was undertaken by the Komatsu Manufacturing Company. The Type 60 has a hull of welded construction with the driver at the front of the hull on the left. The armament is mounted to the right and rear of the driver's position. The engine is at the rear of the hull. Suspension is of the torsion-bar type and consists of five road wheels, with the drive sprocket at the front and the idler at the rear. There are three track-return rollers. The vehicle is armed with two 106mm recoilless rifles built by the Japan Steel Works. These have two positions, low and high. When in the low position, the guns' traverse is limited to 10° left and 10° right, and they can be elevated from −5° to +10°. When the mount is raised the guns have a traverse of 30° left and 30° right and can be elevated from −20° to +15°. On the right re-coilless rifle is a .5in ranging machine-gun. The commander, who also acts as the gunner, first aims the recoilless rifles at the target using a standard optical sight; once the weapons are lined up he fires a burst from the ranging machine-gun; if this strikes the target he then knows that the weapons are correctly lined up, and can then fire the recoilless rifles. Only 10 rounds of High-Explosive Anti-Tank (or High Explosive when the vehicle is being used in the infantry support role) are carried. Once these have been fired the vehicle pulls back to the rear to be resupplied with further ammunition. The vehicle can ford to a maximum depth of 2ft 8in (0.8m). It has no NBC equipment or night-vision equipment. Late production Type 60 self-propelled recoilless rifles are powered by a 150hp diesel.

Below: The Type 60 self-propelled recoilless gun was developed in the 1950s and entered service in 1960. Production was completed in 1979 by which time some 250 vehicles had been built for the Japanese Ground Self-Defence Force.

Type 61 Main Battle Tank

Type 61, Type 67 AVLB, Type 70 ARV and Type 67 AEV
Country of origin: Japan.
Crew: 4
Armament: One 90mm gun; one .3in M1919A4 machine-gun co-axial with main armament; one .5in M2 anti-aircraft machine-gun.
Armour: 64mm (2.52in) maximum.
Dimensions: Length (overall) 26ft 10½in (8.19m); length (hull) 20ft 8in (6.3m); width 9ft 8in (2.95m); height including AA MG 10ft 4in (3.16m).
Weight: Combat 77,162lbs (35,000kg).
Ground pressure: 13.5lb/in² (0.95kg/cm²).
Engine: Mitsubishi Type 12 HM 21 WT 12-cylinder diesel developing 600hp at 2,100rpm.
Performance: Road speed 28mph (45km/h); range 124 miles (200km); vertical obstacle 2ft 3in (0.685m); trench 8ft 2in (2.489m); gradient 60 per cent.
History: Entered service with Japanese Self-Defence Force (Army) in 1962 and still in service.

In appearance the Type 61 has a number of features of the American M47 medium tank, which the Japanese tested in small numbers in the early

1950s. The hull of the Type 61 is of all-welded construction, but the glacis plate can be removed for maintenance purposes. The driver is seated at the front of the hull on the right. The turret is cast, with the commander and gunner on the right and the loader on the left. A stowage box is mounted at the rear of the turret bustle. The engine and transmission are at the rear of the hull. The Japanese have always favoured diesel engines as these have a number of advantages over petrol engines, including low fuel consumption and much reduced fire hazard. The engine is air-cooled and turbocharged. The suspension is of the torsion-bar type and consists of six road wheels, with the drive sprocket at the front and the idler at the rear. There are three track-return rollers. The Type 61 is armed with a 90mm gun built in Japan, and there is a .3in machine-gun mounted co-axially with the main armament. The gun is elevated and traversed hydraulically, with manual controls for use in an emergency. An M2 Browning machine-gun is mounted on the commander's cupola for anti-aircraft defence and this can be aimed and fired from within the cupola. The tank can ford to a depth of 3ft 3in (0.99m) without preparation, but there is no provision for the installation of a schnorkel for deep fording operations. Recently some tanks have been provided with both infra-red driving lights and an infra-red searchlight for night operations. Compared with other tanks of the early 1960s such as the Leopard and AMX-30, the Type 61 is undergunned, but it should be remembered that it was designed to meet Japanese rather than European requirements. The weight and size of the tank had to be kept within certain dimensions as the tank has to be able to be carried on Japanese railways, which pass through numerous narrow tunnels. There are three basic variants of the Type 61 MBT. The bridgelayer is called the Type 67 Armoured Vehicle Launched Bridge, and has a scissors-type bridge which unfolds over the forward part of the hull. This model weighs 36.4 tons (37,000kg) and has a crew of three. Armament consists of a single .3in machine-gun. The recovery version is known as the Type 70 Armoured Recovery Vehicle. On this vehicle the turret is replaced by a small flat-sided superstructure. An 'A' frame is pivoted on this to lift tank components. A dozer blade is provided at the front of the hull. The ARV has a crew of four and a loaded weight of 34.45 tons (35,000kg). Armament consists of a .3in and a .5in machine-gun and an 81mm mortar. Finally there is an Armoured Engineer Vehicle known as the Type 67. This weighs 34.45 tons (35,000kg) and has a crew of four.

Left: The Type 61 was the first tank to be developed in Japan after the end of World War II and entered service with the Japanese Ground Self Defence Force in 1962. It remains in service but has been supplemented by the Type 74 MBT, also developed by the Mitsubishi company.

Type 63 Light Tank

Country of origin: China.
Crew: 4.
Armament: One 85mm gun; one 7.62mm machine-gun co-axial with main armament; one 12.7mm anti-aircraft machine-gun.
Armour: 0.4–0.5in (10–14mm).
Dimensions: Length (with armament) 26ft 10in (8.2m); length (hull) 22ft 8in (6.91m); width 10ft 2in (3.1m); height (turret roof) 7ft 2in (2.19m).
Weight: (combat) 35,280–39,690lbs (16,000–18,000kg).
Engine: 6-cylinder diesel developing 240hp.
Performance: Road speed 25mph (40kmh); range 149 miles (240km); vertical obstacle 3ft 3ins (1m); trench 9ft 2ins (2.8m); gradient 60 per cent.
History: Entered service with the Chinese Army in 1960s. In service with China, Pakistan, Sudan, Tanzania and Vietnam.
(Note: the above specification and designation is provisional).

The Type 63 is a development of the Soviet-supplied PT-76 light amphibious tank and is essentially a Type 60 with a new turret armed with an 85mm gun. The type 63 has been used in combat on a number of occasions including the Vietnam war, the 1971 Indo-Pakistani war and during the Chinese invasion of Vietnam in 1979.

The hull of the Type 63 is all of welded steel construction and is divided up into three compartments, driver's at the front, fighting in the centre and the engine at the rear. The driver is seated on the left side of the hull and has a single piece hatch cover that opens to the left and periscopes for observation with the hatch in the closed position. To his right is probably ammunition stowage. The other three crew members are seated in the turret. The commander and gunner are seated on the left and the loader seated on the right. The commander's hatch opens forwards and the loader's hatch to the rear. The engine and transmission are at the rear and the suspension is of the

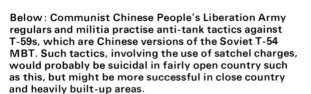

Below: Communist Chinese People's Liberation Army regulars and militia practise anti-tank tactics against T-59s, which are Chinese versions of the Soviet T-54 MBT. Such tactics, involving the use of satchel charges, would probably be suicidal in fairly open country such as this, but might be more successful in close country and heavily built-up areas.

torsion bar type and consists of six rubber tyred road wheels with the idler at the front and drive sprocket at the rear; there are no track return rollers. The Type 63 is fully amphibious and is propelled in the water by two water-jets mounted at the rear of the hull.

Another major improvement of the Type 63 on the original Soviet vehicle is its fire power as the main armament consists of an 85mm rather than a 76mm gun which is also thought to be installed in the Type 62 light tank. This is believed to be a development of the Type 56 field gun (which is a copy of the Soviet D-44). If this assumption is correct the following types of fixed ammunition can be fired: APHE with the projectile weighing 20.5lbs (9.3kg) which will penetrate 4.01in (102mm) of armour at an incidence of 0° at a range of 1094 yards (1000m), HE with the projectile weighing 20.94lbs (9.5kg), and HVAP with the projectile weighing 11.02lbs (5kg); this will penetrate 5.1in (130mm) of armour at a range of 1094 yards (100m). A 7.62mm machine-gun is mounted co-axially to the right of the main armament and mounted on the loader's station is a Type 54 12.7mm heavy machine-gun (the Soviet M1938/46 DShK made in China).

Since the 1960s China has been manufacturing a copy of the Soviet T-54 under the designation of the T-59, and quantities of this tank have also been supplied to many other countries including Albania, Congo, Kampuchea, North Korea, Pakistan, Sudan, Tanzania, and Vietnam. It is most probable that the T-59 has now been succeeded in production by a more modern tank. The Chinese have also built another light tank called the Type 62 which is a scaled down T-59 and weighs about 46,305lbs (21,000kg).

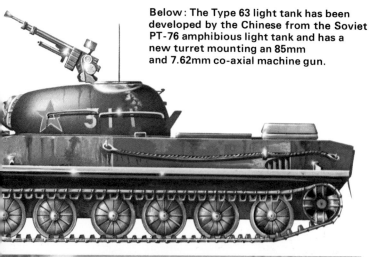

Below: The Type 63 light tank has been developed by the Chinese from the Soviet PT-76 amphibious light tank and has a new turret mounting an 85mm and 7.62mm co-axial machine gun.

Type 74 Main Battle Tank

Country of origin: Japan.
Crew: 4.
Armament: One 105mm L7 series gun; one 7.62mm machine-gun co-axial with the main armament; one .5in anti-aircraft machine-gun; six smoke dischargers.
Armour: Classified.
Dimensions: Length (gun forward) 30ft 10in (9.41m); length (hull) 22ft 6in (6.85m); width 10ft 5in (3.18m); height (with anti-aircraft machine-gun) 8ft 10in (2.675m) at a ground clearance of 2ft 2in (0.65m).
Weight: Combat 83.776lbs (38,000kg).
Ground pressure: 12lb/in² (0.85kg/cm²).
Engine: Mitsubishi 10ZF Model 21 WT 10-cylinder air-cooled diesel developing 750bhp at 2,200rpm.
Performance: Maximum road speed 33mph (53kmh); range 186 miles (300km); vertical obstacle 3ft 3in (1m); trench 8ft 10in (2.7m); gradient 60 per cent.
History: Entered service with the Japanese Self-Defence Force (Army) in 1973 and still in production. *continued* ▶

Right: First prototype of the Type 74 was called the STB-1 and featured automatic loader for the 105mm main armament and a 12.7mm anti-aircraft machine gun which could be aimed and fired by the commander from within the turret.

Above: Type 74 MBT is manufactured by Mitsubishi Heavy Industries near Tokyo and is armed with the British designed 105mm L7 type rifled tank gun which is manufactured in Japan under licence.

The Japanese realised in the early 1960s that the Type 61 would not meet its requirements for the 1980s, so in 1962 design work commenced on a new main battle tank. The first two prototypes, known as STB-1s, were completed at the Maruko works of Mitsubishi Heavy Industries in late 1969. Further prototypes, the STB-3 and the STB-6, were built before the type was considered ready for production. The vehicle entered production at the new tank plant run by Mitsubishi Heavy Industries at Sagamihara in 1973, and the first order was for 280 tanks. The Type 74 has not been exported as at the present time it is the policy of the Japanese government not to export arms of any type. The layout of the tank is conventional, with the driver at the front of the hull on the left and the other three crew members in the turret. The commander and gunner are on the right and the loader is on the left. The engine and transmission are at the rear of the hull. The suspension is of the hydro-pneumatic type and consists of five road wheels, with the drive sprocket at the rear and the idler at the front. There are no track-return rollers. The suspension can be adjusted by the driver to suit the type of ground being crossed. When crossing a rocky, broken area, for example, the suspension would be adjusted to give maximum ground clearance. This clearance can be adjusted from a minimum of 8in (.2m) to a maximum of 2ft 1½in (0.65m). It can also be used to give the tank a tactical advantage : when the tank is on a reverse slope, the suspension can be lowered at the front and increased at the rear so that the main armament is depressed further than normal. The only other tank in service with this type of suspension is the Swedish S tank, which has to have this type of suspension as the gun is fixed to the hull. This type of suspension was also used on the American T95 and German/American MBT-70 tanks, but both these projects were cancelled. The Type 74 is armed with the British 105mm L7 series rifled tank gun, built under licence in Japan. A 7.62mm machine-gun is mounted co-axial with the main armament. The main gun has an elevation of −6.5° and a

Above: One of the more interesting features of the Type 74 MBT is its hydropneumatic suspension which enables the driver to adjust the ground clearance to suit the type of ground being crossed. In addition, when the tank is firing on a reverse slope suspension can be raised at the front and lowered at the rear to give the 105mm gun a depression of −12.5° (normal depression is −6.5°).

depression of +9.5° and using the hydropneumatic suspension an elevation of +15° and a depression of −12.5° can be obtained. The fire-control system includes a laser rangefinder and a ballistic computer, both of which are produced in Japan. Some 51 rounds of 105mm ammunition are carried. Prototypes had an automatic loader, but this would have cost too much to install in production tanks. A .5in M2 anti-aircraft machine-gun is mounted on the roof. On the prototypes this could be aimed and fired from within the turret, but this was also found to be too expensive for production vehicles. Three smoke dischargers are mounted on each side of the turret. The tank is provided with infra-red driving lights and there is also an infra-red searchlight to the left of the main armament. The Type 74 can ford to a maximum depth of 3ft 3in (1m) without preparation, although a schnorkel enabling it to ford to a depth of 6ft 6in (2m) can be fitted. All tanks are provided with an NBC system. In designing the Type 74 MBT the Japanese have sought, and managed, to combine the best features of modern tank design within a weight limit of 37.6 tons (38,000kg). There is only one variant of the Type 74 at the present time, which is the Type 78 Armoured Recovery Vehicle; this is provided with a hydraulically operated crane, winch and a dozer blade at the front of the hull. Currently under development is a new MBT to replace the Type 74 in production in the late 1980s. This has the development designation of the STC and prime contractor for the chassis is Mitsubishi Heavy Industries.

Type 75 155mm
Self-propelled Howitzer

Country of origin: Japan.
Crew: 6.
Armament: One 155mm howitzer; one 12.7mm anti-aircraft machine-gun.
Armour: Classified.
Dimensions: Length (with armament) 25ft 6in (7.79m); length (hull) 21ft 9in (6.64m); width 10ft 1in (3.09m); height (turret roof) 8ft 4in (2.545m).
Weight: (combat) 55,686lbs (25,300kg).
Ground pressure: 0.64kg/cm².
Engine: Mitsubishi 6ZF 6 cylinder diesel developing 450hp at 2200rpm.
Performance: Road speed 29mph (47kmh); range 186 miles (300km); vertical obstacle 2ft 3in (0.7m); trench 8ft 2in (2.5m); gradient 60 per cent.
History: Entered service with Japanese Self Defence Force (Army) in 1977. Still in production.

The first self-propelled artillery to be used by the Japanese Ground Self Defence Force in the post Second World War period was introduced into service in 1965 when 30 105mm M52A1 and ten 155mm M44A1 self-propelled howitzers were procured from the United States. In 1967 development of a 105mm self-propelled howitzer commenced in Japan with Komatsu being responsible for the hull and the Japan Steel Works being responsible for the turret and main armament. This was eventually standardised as the Type 74 105mm self-propelled howitzer, but only 20 were built between 1975 and 1978 as it was decided to concentrate funding on the more effective 155mm weapon.

In 1969 the development of a 155mm self-propelled howitzer had started in Japan with Mitsubishi Heavy Industries being responsible for the turret and Nihon Seiko Jyo/Japan Iron Works being responsible for the turret and main armament. The first two prototypes were completed in 1971/72 and the vehicle was subsequently standardised as the Type 75 self-propelled howitzer. Production commenced shortly afterwards. Mitsubishi Heavy Industries manufacture the hull and also carry out final assembly and testing before delivering the complete system to the Army. In appearance the Type 75 is very similar to the American 155mm M109A1 self-propelled howitzer, but the Japanese model has a slightly longer range.

The hull and turret of the Type 75 are of all welded aluminium construction with the driver seated at the front of the hull with the engine to his left and the

Below: In appearance the Type 75 155mm SPH is similar to the American 155mm M109A1 but the Japanese weapon has a higher rate of fire (6rpm for three minutes) and a slightly longer range.

Above: The Type 75 155mm SPH was designed by Mitsubishi Heavy Industries, Nihon Seiko Jyo and the Japan Iron Works.

turret at the very rear of the hull. Doors are provided in the rear of the hull for ammunition resupply purposes and there are also hatches and doors in the turret. The suspension is of the torsion bar type and consists of six rubber tyred road wheels with the drive sprocket at the front and the last road wheel acting as the idler; there are no track return rollers.

Main armament consists of a long barrelled 155mm howitzer which is provided with a double baffle muzzle brake and a fume extractor, and when travelling the howitzer is normally held in position by a travelling lock. The howitzer fires a Japanese HE projectile to a maximum range of 20,786 yards (19,000m) or an American projectile to a maximum range of 16,410 yards (15,000m). Elevation is from −5° to +65° and the turret can be traversed through a full 360°. Both elevation and traverse are hydraulic with manual controls provided for emergency use.

An unusual feature of the Type 75 is the loading system. In the rear of the turret are two drums, each of which holds nine projectiles, and these, together with the extendable loading tray and the power operated rammer, enable 18 rounds to be fired in three minutes before the two drum magazines have to be reloaded. The latter can be accomplished from inside or outside the vehicle. A total of 28 155mm projectiles are carried plus the necessary bagged charges and fuses.

A 12.7mm machine-gun is pintle-mounted on the roof for anti-aircraft defence, and is provided with a small shield and a total of 1000 rounds of ammunition. The Type 75 is fitted with an NBC system and infra-red night driving equipment and can ford to a depth of 4ft 3ins (1.3m) without preparation.

Vickers Main Battle Tank

Mk 1, Mk 2, Mk 3, Mk 4 and ARV
Country of origin: Britain.
Crew: 4.
Armament: One 105mm gun; one .3in machine-gun co-axial with main armament; one .3in anti-aircraft machine-gun; one .5in ranging machine-gun; 12 smoke dischargers.
Armour: 80mm (3.16in) maximum.
Dimensions: Length (including main armament) 31ft 11in (9.728m); length (hull) 26ft (7.92m); width 10ft 5in (3.168m); height (to commander's cupola) 8ft 8in (2.64m).
Weight: Combat 85,098lbs (38,600kg).
Ground pressure: 12.37lb/in^2 (0.87kg/cm^2).
Engine: Leyland L.60 Mk.4B six-cylinder multi-fuel engine developing 650bhp at 2,670rpm.
Performance: Road speed 35mph (56km/h); range 300 miles (480km); vertical obstacle 3ft (0.914m), trench 8ft (2.438m); gradient 60 per cent.
History: Entered service with the Indian Army in 1965, Kuwait in 1971 and Kenya (Mk 3) in 1979. Still being built in India (Mk 1) and Britain (Mk 3).

In the 1950s it was decided to set up a tank plant in India and teams were sent abroad to select a design which would meet the requirements of the Indian Army. The Vickers design was successful and in August 1961 a licensing contract was signed. Two prototypes were completed in 1963, one being retained by Vickers and the other being sent to India in 1964. Meanwhile plans were being drawn up for a factory to be built near Madras. Vickers delivered some complete tanks to India before the first Indian tank was completed early in 1969. These first tanks had many components from England, but over the years the Indian content of the tank has steadily increased and today the Indians build over 90 per cent of the tank themselves. Production has now passed the thousand mark, and the tank gave a good account of itself in the last Indian-Pakistani conflict. The Indians call the tank *Vijayanta* (Victorious). In designing the tank, Vickers sought to strike the best balance between armour, mobility and firepower within the limits of a tank weighing 38 tons (38,610kg). The layout of the tank is conventional. The driver is seated at the front of the hull on the right with ammunition stowage to his left, and the other three crew members are located in the turret: the commander and gunner to the right and the loader to the left. The engine and transmission are at the rear of the hull. The engine and transmission are the same as those used in the Chieftain MBT. The suspension is of the torsion-bar type and consists of six road wheels with the drive sprocket at the rear and the idler at the front, there being three track-return rollers. The Vickers MBT is armed with the standard 105mm L7 series rifled tank gun, this having an elevation of +20° and a depression of −7°, traverse being 360°. A .3in machine-gun is mounted co-axially with the main armament and a similar weapon is mounted on the commander's

Right: The Mk1 Vickers MBT is being built at Madras in India for the Indian Army who call it the Vijayanta. By 1979 some 1,000 had been built in India and production was continuing. Main armament consists of the well tried 105mm L7 series gun which is also made under licence in India and is installed in many other modern tanks.

cupola. Six smoke dischargers are mounted each side of the turret. Some 44 rounds of 105mm and 3,000 rounds of .3in machine-gun ammunition are carried. The main armament is aimed with the aid of the ranging machine-▶

Above: The latest production model of the Vickers MBT is the Mk3 which is currently being built at Elswick for the Kenyan Army. It has many improvements including a new all cast turret and a laser rangefinder.

Above: The Vickers MBT Mk1 on the firing ranges. The 105mm gun is aimed in the Mk1 version by a 12.7mm ranging MG mounted co-axial with the main armament, and fires in bursts of three rounds.

Above: Vickers MBT Mk1 with General Motors 720bhp turbo-charged diesel, new commander's cupola and thermal sleeve for 105mm gun.

gun method, which has been used so successfully in the Centurion tank with the 105mm gun. The gunner lines up the gun with the target and fires a burst from the .5in ranging machine-gun, and can follow the burst as the rounds are all tracer. If they hit the target he knows that the gun is correctly aimed and he can then fire the main armament. Some 600 rounds of ranging machine-gun ammunition are carried. Two types of main calibre ammunition are used: HESH (High Explosive Squash Head) and APDS (Armour-Piercing Discarding Sabot). A GEC-Marconi stabilisation system is fitted, and this enables the gun to be aimed and fired whilst the vehicle is moving. The model of the tank used by India and Kuwait is the Vickers MBT Mk.1. There was to have been a Mk.2, with four launchers for the British Aircraft Corporation Swingfire ATGW. Vickers Elswick facility is currently producing the Vickers Main Battle Tank Mk 3 for Kenya. This model has a redesigned turret with a cast front which gives increased ballistic protection, Barr and Stroud laser range finder, new commander's cupola which enables him to load, aim and fire his 7.62mm GPMG from within the turret, and a General Motors 12V-71T turbo-charged diesel which develops 720bhp at 2500rpm. The Mk 3 has a maximum road speed of 56km/h and a range of 600km. Optional equipment for the Mk 3 includes passive night vision equipment, deep wading and flotation equipment, full air filtration and pressurisation, heater, fire-control computer, contra-rotating gear for the commander's cupola, fire detection equipment and the replacement of the co-axial 7.62mm MG by a 12.7mm MG.

X1A2 Medium Tank

Country of origin: Brazil.
Crew: 3.
Armament: One 90mm gun; one 7.62mm machine gun co-axial with main armament; one 12.7mm anti-aircraft machine gun; six smoke dischargers.
Armour: Classified.
Dimensions: Length (with armament) 23ft 3in (7.1m); length (hull) 21ft 4in (6.5m); width 8ft 6in (2.6m); height (turret top) 8ft 2.45m).
Weight: (combat) 41,895lbs (19,000kg).
Ground pressure: 0.63kg/cm².
Engine: Scania DS-11 6 cylinder diesel developing 300hp at 2200rpm.
Performance: Road speed 34mph (55kmh); range 466 miles (750km); vertical obstacle 2ft 3in (0.7m); trench 6ft 10in (2.1m); gradient 70 per cent.
History: In production. In service with Brazilian Army.

The X1A2 is an entirely new tank in production for the Brazilian Army by Bernardini of São Paulo. It does incorporate features of the earlier X1A and X1A1 tanks, but these were essentially rebuilds of the American M3A1 Stuart light tank, some 200 of which were supplied by the US over 30 years ago.

The hull is all of welded construction and is divided up into three compartments, driver's at the front, fighting in the centre and the engine at the rear. The driver is seated on the left side with ammunition stowed to his right.

The two other crew members are seated in the all welded steel turret, the commander on the left and the gunner on the right, both with a single piece hatch cover that opens to the rear and vision devices. The engine is made under licence in Brazil and is coupled to a manual transmission with three forward and one reverse gear. The suspension is of the vertical volute type and each side having three bogies each with two road wheels with the drive sprocket at the front, idler at the rear and three tank return rollers that support the inside of the track only.

Main armament consists of a 90mm gun which has a double baffle muzzle brake; this fires an HEAT projectile weighing 8.04lbs (3.65kg) with a muzzle velocity of 831 yards a second (760 metres a second), which will penetrate 12in (320mm) of armour at an incidence of 0°, and an HE projectile weighing 12.56lbs (5.7kg) with a muzzle velocity of 711 yards a second (650 metres a second). Mounted co-axial with the main armament is a 7.62mm machine gun and mounted on the turret roof is a 12.7mm anti-aircraft machine gun. A total of 66 rounds of 90mm, 2500 rounds of 7.62mm and 750 rounds of 12.7mm ammunition are carried. Three electrically operated smoke dischargers are mounted either side of the turret. Optional equipment includes the replacement of the 90mm gun with a 105mm gun, the installation of a laser rangefinder, infra-red night vision equipment and an air-conditioning system. The X1A2 has no amphibious capability although it can ford to a depth of 4ft 3in (1.3m).

Below: The X1A2 tank has been developed for the Brazilian Army, and it incorporates many features of earlier tanks.

XM1 Abrams Main Battle Tank

Country of origin: United States of America.
Crew: 4.
Armament: One 105mm M68 gun; one 7.62mm machine-gun co-axial with main armament; one 0.5in machine-gun on commander's cupola; one 7.62mm machine-gun on loader's hatch (see text).
Armour: Classified.
Dimensions: Length (gun forwards) 32ft (9.766m); length (hull) 26ft (7.918m); width 12ft (3.655m); height (to top of turret) 9ft 6in (2.89m).
Weight: Combat 117,724lbs (53,390kg).
Engine: Avco Lycoming AGT-T 1500 HP-C turbine developing 1,500hp.
Performance: Road speed 45mph (72.4km/h); range 280 miles (450km); vertical obstacle 4ft 1in (1.244m); trench 9ft (2.743m); gradient 60 per cent.
History: Entered production in 1979 for the United States Army, and entered service in 1980.

In June 1973 contracts were awarded to both the Chrysler Corporation (which builds the M60 series) and the Detroit Diesel Allison Division of the General Motors Corporation (which built the MBT-70) to build prototypes of a new tank designated M1, and later named the Abrams tank. These tanks were handed over to the US Army for trials in February 1976. In November 1976 it was announced after a four-month delay that the Chrysler tank would be placed in production. Production commenced at the Lima Army Modification Centre at Lima in 1979 with first production M1s being completed early in 1980. When production of the M60 is completed at Detroit Tank Arsenal early in the 1980s, this will also become available for production of the XM1. The United States Army has a requirement for 7,251 XM1s.

The M1 has a hull and turret of the new British Chobham Armour, which is claimed to make the tank immune to attack from both missiles and tank guns. Its crew consists of four, the driver at the front, the commander and gunner on the right of the turret, and the loader on the left. The main armament consists of a standard 105mm gun developed in Britain and

Below: The M1 MBT is being manufactured at the Lima Tank Plant in Lima, which is run by the Chrysler Corporation. Production of the M1 will also start at Detroit Arsenal in 1982/83.

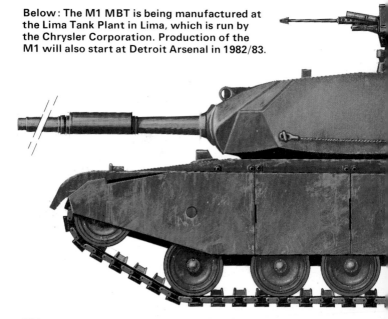

produced under license in the United States and a 7.62mm machine-gun is mounted co-axially with the main armament. A 0.5in machine-gun is mounted at the commander's station and a 7.62mm machine-gun at the loader's station. A total of 55 rounds of 105mm, 1,000 rounds of 0.5in and 11,400 rounds of 7.62mm machine-gun ammunition are carried. The main armament can be aimed and fired on the move. The gunner first selects the ▶

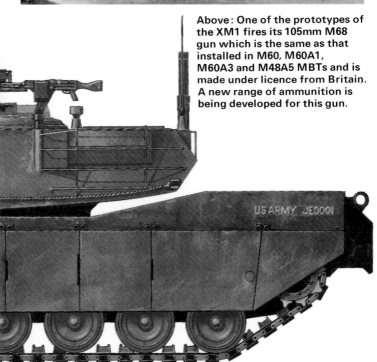

Above: One of the prototypes of the XM1 fires its 105mm M68 gun which is the same as that installed in M60, M60A1, M60A3 and M48A5 MBTs and is made under licence from Britain. A new range of ammunition is being developed for this gun.

Below: One of the prototypes of the XM1 (Abrams) is put through its paces at Aberdeen Proving Ground in Maryland. First production tanks were delivered to the US Army early in 1980 and the Army hopes to have some 7,000 M1s in service by the late 1980s.

Above: Head-on view of one of the prototypes of the XM1 showing the well sloped turret and thick glacis plate. The armour of the XM1 is believed to be based on the British-developed Chobham.

target, and then uses the laser range-finder to get its range and depresses the firing switch. The computer makes the calculations and adjustments required to ensure a hit.

The fuel tanks are separated from the crew compartment by armored bulkheads and sliding doors are provided for the ammunition stowage areas. The suspension is of the torsion-bar type with rotary shock absorbers. The tank can travel across country at a speed of 35mph (56km/h) and accelerate from 0 to 20mph (0 to 32km/h) in six seconds, and this will make the M1 a difficult tank to engage on the battlefield. The M1 is powered by a turbine developed by Avco Lycoming, running on a variety of fuels including petrol, diesel and jet fuel. All the driver has to do is adjust a dial in his compartment. According to the manufacturers, the engine will not require an overhaul until the tank has travelled between 12,000 to 18,000 miles (19,312 to 28,968km), a great advance over existing tank engines. This engine is coupled to an Allison X 1100 transmission with four forward and two reverse gears. Great emphasis has been placed on reliability and maintenance, and it is claimed that the complete engine can be removed for replacement in under 30 minutes.

The M1 is provided with an NBC system and a full range of night-vision equipment for the commander, gunner and driver. It is anticipated that M1s produced from 1984 will be fitted with the West German 120mm Rheinmetall smooth-bore tank gun which is to be manufactured under licence in the United States. The gun is also installed in the Leopard 2 MBT which entered service with the German Army in 1979–80.

It is not often realized that there are hundreds of sub contractors to a major program such as a tank. On the Chrysler M1 there are eight major subcontractors: the government for the armament, Avco-Lycoming for the engine, Cadillac Gage for the turret drive and the stabilization system, the Control Data Corporation for the ballistic computer, the Detroit Diesel Allison Division of General Motors for the transmission and the final drive, the Hughes Aircraft Company for the laser rangefinder, the Kollmorgen Corporation for the gunner's auxiliary sight and the Singer Kearfott Division for the line-of-sight data link.

Above: Mounted co-axial with the main armament is a 7.62mm M240 machine gun while a similar weapon is mounted at the loader's station, the commander has a 12.7mm M2 AA MG.

During trials with XM1 prototypes a number of deficiencies have come to light, especially with the gas turbine engine. In 68,500 miles of testing, problems caused 47 engine failures, but 6,482 miles of intensive testing on refurbished tanks threw up only one engine failure, apparently due to human error. There are three XM1s under tests, which are particularly gruelling: according to *Armed Forces Journal*, each tank will put on 4,000 miles in six months whereas, by comparison, US Army M60s in Europe put on only about 800 to 1,000 miles a year.

Look out for these other
SUPER-VALUE GUIDES!

* Each has 160 fact-filled pages

* Each is colorfully illustrated with action photographs and technical drawings

* Each contains concisely presented data and accurate descriptions of major international weapons

* Each represents terrific value

Following soon:
Illustrated guides to

German, Italian and Japanese
FIGHTERS AND ATTACK AIRCRAFT
of World War II

BOMBERS
of World War II

detailing the exciting combat aircraft that fought in the most ferocious war in history

. . . . thousands of facts and figures
. . . . hundreds of action photos, many in color
. . . . superb color profiles depicting unit markings
. . . . highly detailed three-view line drawings

Your military library will be incomplete without them.

PRINTED IN BELGIUM BY

proost
INTERNATIONAL BOOK PRODUCTION